THE FUTURE OF YOUR ONLY CHILD

ALSO BY CARL PICKHARDT

The Connected Father:
Understanding Your Unique Role and
Responsibilities During Your Child's Adolescence

For his other books, see: www.carlpickhardt.com

THE FUTURE OF YOUR ONLY CHILD

*How to Guide Your Child to
a Happy and Successful Life*

Carl E. Pickhardt, Ph.D.

palgrave
macmillan

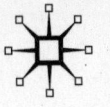

Unless otherwise attributed, all quotations used are fictional, created to reflect concerns similar in kind to those that clients have expressed to me in counseling over the years. Any resemblance to real persons or situations is purely coincidental.

First published in 2008 by
PALGRAVE MACMILLAN™
175 Fifth Avenue, New York, N.Y. 10010 and
Houndmills, Basingstoke, Hampshire, England RG21 6XS.
Companies and representatives throughout the world.

PALGRAVE MACMILLAN is the global academic imprint of the Palgrave Macmillan division of St. Martin's Press, LLC and of Palgrave Macmillan Ltd. Macmillan® is a registered trademark in the United States, United Kingdom and other countries. Palgrave is a registered trademark in the European Union and other countries.

ISBN-13: 978-1-4039-8417-3
ISBN-10: 1-4039-8417-4

Library of Congress Cataloging-in-Publication Data

Pickhardt, Carl E., 1939-
    The future of your only child : how to guide your child to a happy and successful life / Carl Pickhardt.
        p.   cm.
    Includes bibliographical references and index.
    ISBN 1–4039–8417–4
    1. Only child.   I. Title.
    HQ777.3.P52   2007
    649'.142—dc22
                                        2007029402

A catalogue record of the book is available from the British Library.

Design by Letra Libre

First edition: March 2008

10 9 8 7 6 5 4 3 2 1

Printed in the United States of America.

To my father and stepmother, both firstborn children in their families, both treated as the only child at the beginning in ways that empowered them for good and ill all their adult lives.

"*The problems which an only child faces are essentially those faced by all human beings. Onliness is at most a complicating factor. Sometimes it makes a problem more difficult of solution. Not seldom it smoothes the way.*"

—*Norma E. Cutts and Nicholas Mosely,*
The Only Child: A Guide for Parents

"*The only child is simply the most exaggerated version of all of us, growing up, alone.*"

—*Deborah Siegel and Daphne Uviller,*
Only Child: Writers on the
Singular Joys and Solitary Sorrows
of Growing Up Solo

CONTENTS

ACKNOWLEDGMENTS

I would like to acknowledge my indebtedness to the authors of books about only children from which I frequently quote. They have provided me with invaluable understanding in trying, yet one more time, to piece together the psychological puzzle of the only child.

Thank you all!

INTRODUCTION

Because they are prone to thinking ahead, being ever mindful of their son's or daughter's future, parents of single children have one paramount concern: "How will our only child turn out?" On the level of aspirations, these parents usually have a clear idea of what they *want* to happen—the nurturing of the child's desire to achieve, for example. However, parents are often unaware of how the unique dynamics of the one-child family combine with parenting practices, and how these interactions result in characteristics common to an adult only child. It is to help parents on this second level of understanding that *The Future of Your Only Child* is written. To some degree, the psychological future of their only child is in their hands.

Reading so far, you may assume that I am either an only child or at least have parented an only child. No. I am not an only child; I am a middle child and the father of four. However, as a psychologist and writer who specializes in the psychology of parenting, the only-child family has been of particular interest to me. Without the competing presence of siblings to complicate interactions, parents and their only child offer a *simplified family setting* in which to observe how family dynamics and parenting practices can impact a child's growth and how child growth can create the foundation for adult functioning.

Children are shaped in their family of origin both by circumstantial events and by the powerful influence of parents. Through the example they offer and treatment they provide, parents contribute much to how the child turns out as an adult. Thus the child who is continually criticized by parents can become an adult who is self-critical or critical of others. The child who is continually encouraged to take on challenges can become an adult who is self-confident and bold. The child who is respectfully listened to by parents can become an adult who is expressive and outspoken. *How parenting is conducted matters.* Like other students of family functioning, I believe that "what parents believe about human life and human fulfillment governs their way of raising children. The ways children are parented forms their core beliefs about themselves. Nothing could be more important."[1]

Although every family has its unique character, certain types of family situations tend to foster specific shaping effects on children. For example, *children from expatriate families* who grow up in host cultures away from home often have issues about where in the world they truly belong.[2] *Children from divorced families* often grow up learning to keep their emotions hidden, having had parents who were preoccupied with dramatically acting out their own.[3] *Children from alcoholic families* often grow up with a heightened need for predictability and consistency, having had parents whose impulsiveness often felt out of control.[4] In common types of families, predictable dynamics can encourage parenting practices that influence the development of psychological characteristics children typically carry into their adult lives.

The Future of Your Only Child is about the shaping power of another type of family—the only-child family in which one or two parents raise a single biological or adopted child. In this unit, the only child is not simply shaped by all he gets from parents; he is also shaped by all he doesn't get—sibling jealousy, comparison, competition, and conflict, for example. What is *not* experienced can have formative effects.

In this family, dynamics and parenting exert their own special influences. I share this conclusion with others who have also written books about only children.

- "*Don't think you can deny your only-child background.* It is what shaped you. You can learn to cope with its effects, but you can't ignore them."[5]
- "The way in which the only child develops is shaped by the same factor that influences all children—that factor is the parents, and it can be said boldly that the effects of parenting are magnified on the only child because there are no other children around to dilute those effects."[6]

Thus common "shaping effects" of being raised as an only child that are discussed in this book include: being *compliant* with social authority, being *concerned* about approval from adults, being the *center* of attention, being *cautious* about risk taking, being *conservative* about making changes, being *committed* to personal values, being *controlling* in significant relationships, being *content* to spend time alone, being *critical* of self and others, and being *conflict over-reactive* or *avoidant*, among many others.

Of course, only children grow up through the same stages of development as children with siblings. Growing up is never an easy task for any child. With every challenge along the way—more independence or responsibility for example—comes some degree of struggle as the child tries to master more than he was able to do before. Trial, error, and recovery describe the learning curve of growing up.

Most children start the process with some degree of attachment to and dependence on parents, separating and differentiating during adolescence, and then gradually gathering enough power through knowledge, experience, and responsibility to finally claim the functional independence that young adulthood requires. During this process, however, certain family dynamics, parenting practices, and developmental challenges or struggles come into play that are accentuated for the only child. It is the *combination* of these forces that tends to shape the psychological characteristics of this child as an adult.

These characteristics are commonly expressed in relationship to herself, with significant others, and in her social world. Just as children with siblings owe some of their challenges to having siblings (rivalries for example), "only children owe some of their struggles to being Onlies."[7] These struggles, of course, do not belong to the child alone. They also belong to those vitally interested parties, her parents, who are trying to figure out how to help their only child happily and effectively manage the challenges that come with growing up as a single child (many of which are described in this book).

Most of these issues I have dealt with in counseling with only children still at home with their parents, and with the family as a whole. In addition, I have counseled adult only children in significant relationships who discover how some ways of defining themselves and treating others that they learned growing up with parents as primary companions usually require adjustment when it comes time to commit to an adult partner. At this juncture, adult only children should not be surprised to discover some unfinished growing up that has yet to be done. "If only children do have common behavior patterns arising from their distinct upbringing, then the people most likely to be exposed to such behavior are their partners."[8]

By anticipating some of these common adult outcomes, parents can prepare their child for life in a caring adult relationship later on. For example, by helping their son or daughter comfortably confront differences and constructively resolve conflict without avoidance or coercion, parents can prepare the adult only child to do so with a partner. Discomfort with conflict from lack of sibling competition is just one common characteristic of many adult only children. (See chapter 8.)

It is important to understand that all the psychological characteristics I describe in this book are susceptible to parental influence and personal change because they are primarily learned. In counseling I have seen people alter characteristics time and again. For example, when parents have let go of excessive worry and undue protection, the only child who, to his regret, was overcautious became more adventurous and confident. I have also seen adult only children who were unhappily wed to making rigid plans, lists, and schedules in order to manage the uncertainties of life learn to "loosen up" after practicing methods leading to more spontaneity, improvisation, and trust in the face of unexpected change. By altering their own behavior, parents can change the shaping influence they assert. By choosing to practice different beliefs and behaviors, adult only children can modify the terms on which they live with themselves, with other people, and with the world.

This is a book about learned characteristics, not unalterable traits. It is about tendencies, not certainties. It is about parental influence, not determination. It is about direction, not destiny. It is about having individual choice, not being a victim of family circumstance. Although supported by psychological investigation that has been done about sibling birth order and about only children, *The Future of Your Only Child* is primarily based on my experience counseling members of only-child families. I cite more books about only children than research articles on the subject because they attempt a deeper understanding and a broader perspective. All the books about only children that are quoted I have found to be extremely sensitive and wise, each in its own way.

The first chapter of *The Future of Your Only Child* summarizes recent demographic trends about only-child families and then briefly reviews some birth order and only-child research. Each of the fifteen subsequent chapters describes one family dynamic in psychological detail. It discusses the shaping forces of parenting practices that can enhance or moderate the influence of that dynamic and provides descriptions of adult only-child outcomes that commonly occur as a function of that dynamic.

Of course, not all of the fifteen dynamics have equal influence on every young only child. Each individual life is affected by many more mediating factors—from genetic to circumstantial to social to cultural—than just being raised as an only child. However, NOW = LATER is the shaping equation upon which this book is based. Parenting *can* make a difference. Childhood experience influences adult functioning. By knowing what dynamics you have to work with in the single child family and what characteristics from growing up often come to describe an adult only child, your parenting practices can help shape the future of your only child.

Finally, let's discard the matter of "only-child guilt." Parents of only children are sometimes accused of spoiling them through parental indulgence and of subjecting them to terminal loneliness because there are no siblings. This accusation is not valid. As psychologist Susan Newman says: "A sibling is not required to help parents raise a happy, well-adjusted child."[9]

But my favorite responses to this charge are found in Ellen Peck's *The Joy of the Only Child*. "Nobody criticizes me for having an only dog or an only husband . . . but I have been warned that [our only child] is sure to face adjustment problems without siblings. I think he would face such problems *with* siblings, given what I have seen in other families."[10] Later she quotes one of her expert sources. "We are often told that only children express a desire to have brothers and sisters. How often does the opposite occur—how often do siblings wish to be onlies?"[11]

Without siblings or with siblings, a child must always adjust to the family's composition. There is no childhood without some complexities at home to be faced and some adversities to be overcome.

So to parents of an only child, and to only children everywhere, I want to say: *Instead of feeling guilty about your family circumstance, be grateful for all the good things that you get to give as parents and to receive as an only child.*

1

BIRTH ORDER AND ONLY-CHILD RESEARCH

Although, for the purposes of this book, the term "only child" refers to a single biological or adopted child in a two-parent or single-parent nuclear family, there are in fact a variety of lesser "only-child" roles in which similar dynamics, parenting practices, and adult outcomes are present.

- The *eldest child* is by birth order an only child until another sibling comes along—*the only child at the outset.* By being a "trial child," the one who introduces parents to parenting and gets first call on their attention, the oldest child is often not inclined to yield her dominant position to younger arrivals (and rivals) on the family scene who gladly testify to how bossy an older brother or sister can be. ("First come, first served," and the eldest child means to keep it that way.)
- *The youngest child* becomes an only child when older siblings have outgrown the family and departed—*the only child left at home.* Now able to capture the undivided attention of the parents, the youngest child offers them their last chance at par-

enting, becoming the one whom they are inclined to indulge and give in to.

- The *special needs child* is an only child in terms of receiving a disproportionate amount of parental time, energy, concern, and resources—*the only child receiving so much extra attention.* Special expenses, special regimens, special therapies, special education, special arrangements and accommodations, and special parental vigilance are required to help the child survive and thrive.
- The *surviving child* becomes an only child after another sibling dies—*the only child left alive.* Grief-stricken over loss and desperate to ensure the safety and well-being of their last living child, parents can become extremely focused on their remaining son or daughter.
- *The gender-favored child* becomes an only child when the distinction of being the sister with all brothers or the brother with all sisters is highly prized—*the only child of that sex.* Doted on and given special treatment, the only girl or only boy can be granted favored status in the family.
- The *star child* becomes an only child when public recognition of personal achievement confers credit on the parents—*the only child to glorify the family.* Extra parental investment in the child, and the exceptions and arrangements made for his or her advancement, create special treatment and status at home.

The experience of the eldest child shall be more fully discussed in this chapter because by birth order, until other siblings arrive, "firstborns whose closest siblings are six or more years younger are functionally similar to only children."[1]

In addition, it is important to understand that the greater the time span between one sibling and the next, the more likely that only-child family dynamics and only-child characteristics will develop. Thus in a family with a ten-year-old and a newborn, each is likely to become accustomed to only-child treatment by the parents.

As for the incidence of parents with a single child, this is becoming an increasingly common family unit in the United States and worldwide.

THE DEMOGRAPHIC TREND

How common is it to have an only child? A few citations describe the incidence of single-child families in this country today.

- "One in five families today has an only child. Back in 1970, the average family had 2.5 children. Today, the average is 1.8."[2]
- "According to census bureau data from 2003, about 20 percent of U.S. children under 18 had no siblings at home."[3]
- "There are currently 20 million single-child families in the U.S. The percentage of American women having only one child has more than doubled in 20 years to almost one quarter. The single-child family is the fastest-growing family in the U.S. and most of Western Europe."[4]

The longer people wait to have children, say until over age thirty, the fewer children they tend to have. The combination of late start and cost considerations contribute to a likely future having more small and single-child families.

- "According to the Census Bureau's 1998 Current Population Survey, a greater percentage of women of all ages are not having children."[5]

Biological, step, adoptive, and foster parenting all require investing time, energy, and resources in supporting and socially preparing the next generation of human life. Parenting is expensive. It is a continuing act of significant self-sacrifice, one that increasing numbers of people in this country are choosing not to make. *The adult trend is not simply to having smaller families, to having a single child, but also to having no children at all.*

Of course, when one includes the Republic of China, with about 1.3 billion people, a country that in 1979 instituted a "one-child policy" to gain control over its ever-growing population, the relatively recent worldwide surge in only-child families becomes enormous. No wonder interest in psychological research into only children has also grown.

The issue addressed in this book is *not* whether being raised as an only child is healthier or unhealthier, better or worse, than being raised among siblings. My point is that the family dynamics, parenting practices, and child development in only-child nuclear families tend to be identifiably *different* than in multiple-child families; they yield a predictable mix of personal characteristics (both strengths and limitations) that are frequently carried into young adulthood. Despite much professional disagreement over whether growing up an "only" makes any developmental difference in shaping individual characteristics and conduct, many investigations of eldest children and only children suggest that these differences do exist.

In writing *The Future of Your Only Child*—in addition to mining over twenty years of consultations with only children and their parents and with adult only children on their own—I have drawn on two other sources for understanding: the psychological literature about birth order and about the only child. This literature has been helpful in my own thinking, and so, throughout this book, I draw on what others have thought and found to support and amplify what I have to say.

BIRTH ORDER RESEARCH AND WRITING

Birth order research theorizes that one's ordinal position among siblings can favor the development of certain psychological characteristics and foster the development of certain patterns of behavior. My interest in birth order is founded on what it has to say about the eldest child, who is an only child for a while. Both eldest and only children function as the first and single child. To be an only child at first creates privilege and standing the child naturally wants to protect; he often continues to act as an only child after a second child arrives.[6] Sometimes parents will describe how the first child initially engages in willful denial of this family change, acting as if the newborn sibling simply isn't there and so no accommodation need be made to this rival for their attention and affection. And many second children, as they grow, will describe how the oldest child continued to rule the family roost.

At first glance, birth order would appear to be a very simple factor to understand. On closer inspection, however, it becomes extremely complex. Embedded in this variable is an enormous array of qualifying conditions and confounding circumstances that some psychologists believe dilute any consistent psychological effect. After all, for family birth order to have a generalized psychological effect, all families would have to be more similar than different, or the enormous diversity among families would have to be overridden by the power of ordinal position among siblings.

Does birth order have a formative effect on people's psychological characteristics? In professional psychology, the debate goes on. Some researchers believe that there is no significant psychological effect.[7] Others vigorously disagree, believing that birth order goes a long way in explaining psychological differences among siblings.[8] I am not deeply enough read to resolve this disagreement, but I do have a position to take in this book, and it is this.

If the question is "Can birth order *completely explain* psychological differences among siblings?" I believe the answer is "No, it cannot." However, if the question is "Can birth order *contribute* to our understanding of psychological differences among siblings?" I believe the answer is "Yes, it often can."

An only child is both a first child and a last child in one—first, and therefore the only chance at parenting most parents will get; and last, because there are no more to come. As with other birth-order positions, determining any consistent psychological significance connected to a firstborn is very elusive, yet psychologists and writers like myself persist in this endeavor. Why?

In counseling, clients frequently assign some shaping influence to their birth order, using it to explain why they became the way they are.

- "Because I was the oldest, my parents were pretty nervous starting out with me, not knowing what to do or afraid of not doing it right. Maybe that's why it's easy to feel anxious when I'm unsure now."
- "Because I was youngest, I had to defend against being picked on by the older kids. Maybe that's why I stand up for myself now."

- "Because I was in the middle, I was often ignored for the other two. Maybe that's why I like being left to myself now."
- "Because I was the only child, I received all my parents' hopes and dreams. Maybe that's why I try so hard not to disappoint people now."

They believe their birth order mattered. Although it may not be a robust statistical predictor of psychological differences in the population at large, birth order is often a very useful clinical variable to explore with individual clients.

Is there any consistent pattern of influence to a particular birth-order position in general? Consider what a few research sources have to say about the psychological characteristics of an eldest child.

COMMON PSYCHOLOGICAL
CHARACTERISTICS OF THE ELDEST CHILD

There is a vast birth-order literature, and I have only skimmed the surface to come up with a few characteristics of the eldest child that are repeatedly mentioned.

Because the firstborn child has only parents in the nuclear family to identify with, and because she receives all the attention and care the parents have to give, she becomes closely wed to following along with what they want and fitting in with them. Consequently, some research findings tend to portray her as a conforming, conservative, and conventional believer in the family order.[9] Since the eldest child is more likely to conscientiously achieve up to parental expectations, laterborns become the children more likely to rebel.[10] An entire book has been devoted to reviewing research about this distinction between the more conformist firstborn and the more rebellious laterborns.

In *Born to Rebel,* science historian Frank Sulloway describes firstborn characteristics that I believe contribute to understanding the only child:[11]

- "Eldest children tend to identify more closely with parents and authority. This well-documented tendency is consistent with the general profile of firstborns as ambitious, conscientious, and achievement orientated. Relative to younger siblings, eldest children are more conforming, conventional, and defensive—attributes that are all negative features of openness to experience." [12]

- "Firstborns are reported to be more self-confident than laterborns . . . firstborns should be more amenable than laterborns to their parents' wishes, values, and standards . . . The tendency for firstborns to excel in school and in other forms of intellectual achievement is consistent with their strong motivation to satisfy parental expectations. Studies have repeatedly found that firstborns are 'more strongly identified with parents and readier to accept their authority.'" [13]
- "Firstborns are described as being more anxious about their status. They are also more emotionally intense than laterborns and slower to recover from upsets . . . Firstborns . . . tend to endorse conventional morality." [14]
- Firstborns are "more conforming, traditional, and closely identified with parents . . . more responsible, achievement orientated, organized, and planful . . . more extraverted, assertive, and likely to exhibit leadership." [15]

It is said that close identification with parents creates a more traditional and less rebellious orientation for the eldest child; I believe this also tends to be true for the only child.

Now consider what a few writers and researchers have to say about the only child.

COMMON CHARACTERISTICS OF THE ONLY CHILD

Let's begin our findings about the only child with a textbook description: "Only children tend to be more like older children in that they enjoy being the center of attention. Because they spend more time in the company of adults, rather than siblings, they tend to mature sooner and to adopt adultlike behaviors earlier in life." [16] This early and unwavering desire to act grown-up plays a significant role in many of the dynamics described in this book, whether in the quality of intimacy in friendship the only child seeks, the level of performance he is ambitious to achieve, the sense of serious responsibility he develops, or in the moral compass that determines the sense of rectitude that directs much of his behavior.

The expert who has conducted and reviewed more research on only children than any other I have found is psychologist Toni Falbo. After reviewing 141 studies of the personality characteristics of only children, she concluded that in most cases only children scored about the same as children with siblings, except in two characteristics where scores were significantly higher—in self-esteem and achievement motivation.[17]

Interviewed in 2004 about the robust nature of this finding, Falbo noted, "These children tend to score slightly higher in verbal ability, go farther in school and have a little bit higher self-esteem."[18]

Another major source of research that includes a focus on only children that I find meaningful is the "family constellation" work of Walter Toman. The profile he describes for the only child in the family constellation fits many characteristics that I further explore in this book.

> An only child has no sibling position. Oldest siblings have been single children for a while but were dethroned when their first sibling arrived. The only child, however, retains his privileged position. His main contacts are his parents... the only child is not or is only indirectly prepared for contacts with peers... At home they learn to command their parents' entire attention... Only children frequently know better than other children how to handle adults, or how to involve them for their own purposes... only children look and act like little adults themselves... There are no other children to identify with... They don't have to share their parents with other children... They want to be in the limelight, under the guidance and protection of older people or people in authority. They strive for recognition for what they want or do not want to do. They can attract "followers" and take on leadership roles for their peers to the degree to which they identify with adults, with authority figures, or with subject matters. Even then, they unconsciously value the understandings of their superiors more than that of those in their charge... On the average... only children have been more poorly prepared for contacts with peers than children with any other sibling position; they prefer contacts with older persons or people in high positions.[19]

Finally, based on their extensive interviews, Jill Pitkeathley and David Emerson propose a test for identifying who is likely to be an only child in a group of people. I find it telling. They write:

Ask yourself who is

- The most responsible person in the group?
- The most organized?
- The most serious?
- The one who is rarely late?
- The one who doesn't like arguments?
- The self-possessed one?

The chances are that the one who is all of these things will be the only child. It's not infallible, but it's pretty reliable as a test.[20]

Research on eldest and only children does suggest that being a single child in the family, at the outset or for always, can psychologically shape the growth of that girl or boy in ways that often result in predictable adult characteristics. The purpose of this book is to examine how this influence can occur in the only-child family. Each subsequent chapter explores one of the fifteen family dynamics I have found salient when counseling with only children, parents of only children, and adult only children. *It is the cumulative force of these dynamics, not the power of any single one, which sets the only-child family experience apart from that in families with multiple children.*

2

ATTENTION

A Matter of Notice

Like each of the fifteen family dynamics described in this book, attention is double-edged—it has the potential to be both strengthening and problematic, and the parental job is to maximize the first and moderate the second as best they can.

Only children benefit from the undivided attention of their parents. It's not just that self-worth is affirmed by positive parental notice. The only child becomes very aware of his character and capacities from the feedback parents constantly provide. In addition, their ever-readiness to pay him attention creates an open stage for showing off what he can do. By performing for this untiring parental audience, he develops a lot of self-confidence. On the problematic side, however, the attention fosters a number of characteristics that can adversely affect his relationships with others now and later—such as undue self-importance, self-concealment, self-consciousness, self-centeredness, and the "only attitude."

What is it like to be the focus of undivided parental attention growing up as an only child? Here is one adult's take on the experience:

You're it. That's the bottom line. If you're the son, you must also be the daughter. If you're the daughter, you must be the son too... You're the hope, the dreams; and you're the one and the only one to blame if it doesn't turn out all right—according, of course, to your parents' definition of "all right." It's not that people with siblings don't experience the same sort of pressure. The difference is that all the pressure, all the focus, is on little old you... It seems to me I spent most of my childhood longing to be neglected... What does only childhood do to a person? I'm certainly self-centered; on the other hand I think I'm less needy of attention than those who experienced the kind of childhood neglect I longed for. I have close friendships, but I want a lot back. I want love from them and often I get only like. I read a lot, a habit I developed in childhood when there was no one to play with... Life as an only child shapes you, but so do a trillion other things.[1]

Part infatuation and part anxiety, there is vigilance in the attention parents give an only child—a combination of watching closely what is happening and watching out for what might occur. In love with this addition to their lives, they also take this new responsibility very seriously. Prone to precaution, they are often inclined to seek medical advice at the infant's earliest sign of discomfort. First time parents are more concerned and less confident, more nervous and less relaxed, than are seasoned parents who've had children before. In multiple-child families, later children tend to become a lesser source of celebration—and of worry, too, as parents learn from past parenting experience and feel more secure.

It is very important to remember that parents with multiple children who have a child die are still left with other children. They remain active parents because their parenting responsibilities continue. This is not so with parents of an only child. Should that child die, not only are attachment to and investment in the child lost, but their entire identity and role as parents as well. This is partly why parents of an only child are so careful, conscientious, and conservative, why they are so protective: They have so much to lose.

The historical data testify to the extreme attention the first and only child is paid. All kinds of records, photographs, and artifacts are meticulously maintained, evidence of the close attention parents gave. Collecting such treasures shows how parents luxuriate in noticing the first and only child. In multiple-child families, data on subsequent children are usually less completely and consistently kept.

"Watch me!" "Hear me!" "Look at what I made!" "See what I can do!" In response to these requests from their first or only child, parents respond with true delight. With parents so attentive and approving it is no wonder the only child plays to their enthusiastic response. At least at the beginning, few are the parents who can resist giving extreme attention to their only child, who loves showing off for this adoring audience.

SELF-WORTH

Every expression of positive parental attention conveys to the only child that he or she is worth paying attention to and so is a direct deposit into the young person's bank of self-esteem. Simply by being paid a lot of attention, most only children come to think well of themselves. This may help explain why only children achieve as well as they do. One psychologist states this case well:

> Studies have demonstrated that only children's better-than-others intellectual performances, especially in the area of verbal ability, are not necessarily related to how smart or well-educated their parents are. In other words, only children don't do as well as they do because they've inherited their IQ from intelligent parents and intelligent parents tend to have smaller families... Their parents *spend time* with them, because without other children, they have more time to spend. They read to their children (only children, much more than others, report being read to as preschoolers). They *talk* to them a lot. And only children, in turn, tend to model their language on grown-ups rather than on other children (and verbal ability is perhaps the strongest predictor of educational success)... And various studies have demonstrated, not surprisingly, that their parents spend more time with them, throughout childhood, than do other parents with their children—according to one analysis, mothers of onlies interact with their children more than twice as much as do mothers of more than one.[2]

People pay attention to what matters to them. In the case of an only child, parents pay a lot of attention because that single son or daughter matters so much. In response, only children tend to view themselves in a host of empowering ways, one of which is the child's enduring sense of being special. On this characteristic of the only child, some writers and adult only children seem to agree.

- "Because only children are treated as special, they feel they are special."[3]
- "An only child is a very special person, both growing up and grown-up."[4]
- One only child explained it this way: "There is something that being an only child gives to you. You get a sense that you're wonderful and special, and you can carry that with you." Another added, "When there's only one, you are told time and time again that you're very special. And you start to think you're very special . . . I think feeling special . . . made me much more motivated. I really don't think about failure very often. I think I can do almost anything I set my mind to."[5]

Due in part to constant parental attention, only children tend to become self-aware, self-valuing, and self-invested. They know who they are, they respect who they are, they feel significant, and they are determined to stay true to this definition of themselves. Being so in touch with themselves is a birthright of the only child. Her capacity for self-interest and for keeping herself good company can make for a rich and satisfying journey through adult life.

Not shy, at least at home, about courting adult attention, the only child is often confident about putting herself forward in the grown-up world, seeking attention to show off accomplishments, demonstrate abilities, and put self-expression on display. This confidence in speaking up and holding forth, especially with adults, is founded on the belief that he has something of interest worth saying. How does he know? On occasions too numerous to remember, parental attention has told him so. The sense of being special and being comfortable communicating with older people creates an enormous advantage for the young adult who is making his way in the world.

Undivided adult focus (attention from parents) and uninterrupted time alone (attention from self) are the twin gifts that come with being an only child. In both cases special valuing is given.

SELF-IMPORTANCE

When nothing about the only child seems to escape her parents' notice, it's easy for her to assume the rest of the world scrutinizes her to the same degree and thus she feels excessively important. Part of becoming an adult only child is accepting that no one, including an adult partner, will ever again give her the devoted, and at times oppressive, degree of attention her parents did. No one will be as fascinated and impressed by her as they were; no one will believe she is quite so special. Getting over the sense of self-importance that comes from basking in their adoringly attentive eyes is part of growing into independent adulthood, neither expecting nor striving for that degree of importance in another relationship again.

One adult only child commented on her adjustment to this realization: "The biggest indulgence was my parent's attention. They always listened to me and acted like everything I had to say was interesting. They made me feel that just being me was good enough. That was great in many ways, but it had a downside. As an adult, I've had to learn again and again that nobody is impressed with me just because I'm Fran."[6] *Many adult only children would have an easier time living with others if they gave up some degree of self-importance.* "First come, first served" is how the only child is treated at home because no additional children compete for parental priority. Growing up being first in line for attention, it is natural to expect that position in adult attachments, an expectation that is usually disabused by a partner who insists on equality. This is often when the adult only child learns to take turns, to wait for someone else, even to put someone else first. This adjustment is not easy. One adult only child described this difficulty well. "What the only child gets, in capital letters, is UNDIVIDED ATTENTION. I still expect it because I always got it from my parents. I don't want anyone to look the other way when I'm talking. If they look away, I'll ask them 'OK, tell me what I said.' That's crazy because you can't expect people to pay attention to you the way your parents did, but that's the way I am. I don't think only children readily give up expecting undivided attention."[7]

One task of adult adjustment, usually accomplished in significant relationships, is learning to get over the importance of oneself and to respect the equal importance of the other person.

SELF-CONCEALMENT

This unrelenting focus of parental attention can also have a discomforting side. Continual adult notice causes the only child to feel oppressively self-aware. In consequence, it's easy for him to feel closely observed and become socially self-conscious on that account, although others are far less interested and attentive than he might suppose. Sometimes parental attention can feel too close for comfort. In the words of one adult only child, "I've heard it said that mothering a child is like watching your heart walk around outside your chest. To my mother, for whom there is only me, I am heart, spleen, and marrow. She is quick to take me at my word. If I'm anxious, she'll find a solution before I know what's wrong. Rarely, if ever, am I allowed to feel uncomfortable in my skin, perhaps because it is her own. More often than not, I relish being the object of such undiluted attention. But sometimes, when the focus becomes too acute, I feel I might catch fire."[8]

One of the great strengths of parents of an only child is their supervision of detail. With multiple children, much can escape parental notice. In addition, some parental resolves are not consistently applied, some good intentions are not carried through, and some requirements are not uniformly enforced, because when managing so many children some slippage is bound to occur. Parents just can't keep up with three children as closely as they can with one. Given this undistracted parental focus, however, the only child can feel constantly under a microscope, sometimes wishing there was another child in the family to direct parental attention elsewhere. "Some only children find the focus of attention almost overwhelming."[9]

Parents need to be mindful that although only children like receiving a lot of notice, even they can reach their limits, particularly during adolescence, when tolerance for parental oversight and surveillance becomes reduced as the desire for freedom for privacy and social independence naturally increases. This creates an ongoing need for parents of an only child to discriminate between paying enough attention and paying too much.

Pay too much, and the adolescent only child can find this level of attention invasive and oppressive, as the following three only children declare.

- "[One adolescent] found that her closeness to her mother also robbed her of privacy. 'It was impossible to have a secret life,' she recalls. 'She always knew what I was doing. I think there tends to be a boundary problem. And because there aren't any other children, a parent doesn't have to respect that boundary.'"[10]
- "I was my parents' entire life outside of work. On the one hand, I received a tremendous amount of personal attention; I liked that. On the other hand, one can't readily hide things from parents. Being the central figure is the same thing I didn't like."[11]
- "Because the focus is on you and you can't afford to put a foot wrong, you are on your guard more yourself as a child. If there's three or four the parents aren't looking all the time and the odd slip can go unnoticed. When the focus is on you, every slip is noticed."[12]

No wonder, come adolescence, that only children will engage in dishonesty with parents to create privacy and secrecy to escape the excessive parental scrutiny. In the words of one: "Because my mother's attention was always on me and I could never hide anything, I learned at an early age that if I was going to win at all I had to become deceitful. I lied and pretended."[13]

One common legacy of growing up as an only child under extremely attentive parents is becoming an adult who, in partnership or marriage, needs sufficient space apart and time alone to preserve adequate privacy.

So what is a parent to do? As one psychologist advises, "Don't constantly scrutinize your child; overlook something he does that you may not like but which may not be important in the scheme of development. If he's been on the phone too long with a friend or stayed up reading too late, pretend you don't notice every now and again. Give your only a sense of privacy and his own identity, something he would automatically get if you were caring for more than one."[14] And understand how constant, close parental attentiveness tends to encourage the child to be self-conscious of her own behavior.

SELF-CONSCIOUSNESS

Evidence of the adult only child's self-consciousness is often found in her eye for the particulars in life. Much more inclined to be precise than to be casual, ordered than disorganized, neat than messy, to do tasks thoroughly than halfway, the adult only child takes the time to keep track of small things, whether they have to do with appearance, possessions, plans, or commitments. "Pay attention to details" describes how many adult only children function, a legacy of parental attention paid them growing up that they learned to pay in turn to themselves and their world. Specifics are supposed to matter, as one adult only child in counseling described it. "I grew up under my parents' close attention, and now I watch myself as closely as they once did me. For instance, I never take a nonprescription drug without thoroughly reading the information about side effects. My mother taught me that. And when I go to a restaurant, I always carefully check the bill to see that I'm not overcharged. That's from my dad. The lesson was to pay close attention to small things so big problems could be avoided. Which I still believe is true, but it's a tiring way to live." No wonder dedication to attention breeds such characteristics as mindfulness, carefulness, and thoroughness in the only child. Attention to details is often a defining quality of an only child who tends to be very observant and can be fussy about how things are done.

It's not just that an only child adjusts to getting a lot of attention, some of which he wants and some he doesn't, but he learns to pay a lot of attention to himself. He feels impelled to monitor how he is doing, laboring under the unblinking eye of his own self-consciousness, and becomes self-centered as a response.

SELF-CENTEREDNESS

Along with the power of parental attention to foster self-consciousness in their only child, there is a companion tendency that the only child can also develop: to become extremely self-centered in relationships, what has been described as "the unified, solitary, self-referential reality of being an only child."[15]

It happens like this. When treated as the primary focus of parental attention, the only child easily comes to treat himself the same way. He experiences the family as a child-centered world meant to revolve around his needs, so he assumes the larger universe does, too. He can become so self-centered in his perception that at times he can't see others, or he only sees others in terms of himself. He starts to understand, evaluate, and respond to whatever is going on around him by how it affects or reflects on him. For example, the third-grade only child who has just been told that his friend has fallen sick and so cannot come over to play this afternoon as planned, has an immediate response: "That spoils my fun!" Of course, this is an age when lots of children may lack immediate empathy for others, but even more so for only children who have a penchant for self-centeredness. From being the center of attention, they can develop a "tendency to judge every situation by how it affects them."[16]

Sensitive to her son's self-centered statement, and wanting to help him be able to move beyond self-preoccupation to concern for others, a mother first asks: "I know that's how *you* feel, but how do think *he* feels?" Then she follows that question with another: "What can you do to help your friend feel better while he's sick?" And together they can make up a care package of activities to drop off at the friend's house.

This tendency to be self-centered in relationships, unless modified in childhood, can carry over into marriage for the adult only child in the form of an *interpersonal blindness.* Consider the husband in couple counseling who, in frustration with his only-child wife, finally declares, "Every time I have a complaint about something bad happening to me, we always end up talking about how it affects you! Can't you see beyond yourself? My life is not all about you. It's about me!" Being so highly self-centered can result in a lack of empathy. Sometimes an adult only child has to practice setting her self aside, has to learn to orbit around someone else's self-interest, and respond to others based on their self-centeredness and not her own. She must learn to see beyond herself. In practical terms, this means taking the time to ask: "Forgetting about myself for the moment, what is the other person telling me about them that I need to understand and respond to?" Some only children need to practice simple listening, the art of paying attention to what the other person is saying. In addition, acts of service, sacrifice, and support can direct the sensitivities of the only child to the welfare of others.

One outcome of acting so self-centered is projecting his own experience onto others, and then reacting to that, causing other people to feel misunderstood, discounted, or ignored.

The good side of all the parental attention is how self-affirming the only child tends to grow. The problematic side is that all the attention can cause the only child to develop a so-called only attitude.

THE "ONLY ATTITUDE"

Ask parents why they have decided to have a single child, and a common response is: "Because one is *enough*." Yes, one is certainly enough to create a family, if you define family as some combination of parent and child. However, what parents don't seem to understand is that having an only child can also be *too much* when parental attention turns into parental absorption that fosters undue self-importance in the child. Thus doted on, the child can come to believe that

- I come first.
- I matter most.
- I should get my way.

Parents beware: Cultivate an only attitude in your young child and, come adolescence, you will have a teenager who rules the home. *The parental challenge is to nurture their only child with undivided positive attention without unwittingly creating an oppressively self-centered presence in the family.*

In multiple-child families, the next child forces parents to make a *second child adjustment* that reduces the preoccupying power of the first and only child. Concentration on one is broken by the plurality of two. No longer able to be absorbed by a single child, parents must now divide their attention between competing siblings, and come to accept that *some* of what they have to give is going to have to be enough for each child. This change liberates parents from their fixation on child number one, and moderates both their expectations about how much they can realistically contribute to each child and how much each child can realistically expect from her parents. From here on, they can never pay as much attention to child number one as they did before, and they can never give to child number two as much as they once exclusively gave to the first. Now parents discover that it's easier saying no when they have two children than when they had only one. In addition, a very important demotion in family identity and status takes place. The firstborn is now reclassified by parents as one of the children ("one of them") and is no longer considered, or can consider herself, as one of the adults ("one of us").

Since this liberation from parental preoccupation and the moderation of parental attention and investment are less likely to occur with an only child (where attention and investment are extreme), it can be helpful to have another child—not literally, but figuratively. Consider some possible strategies. Develop, as an individual or couple, an interest to which your only child must accommodate. Your only child will have to do without your company while you spend time on a competing source of enjoyment and attention. For example, start that daily exercise program you have been putting off because it took time from parenting, or both of you can go out on a weekly date and leave your child attended by a sitter at home. Responsible selfishness decrees that to support the child parents must adequately invest in themselves individually and in the preservation of their union. *Rundown parents in a strained marriage create an insecure family for their only child.*

Do not sacrifice individual well-being and that of the marriage on the altar of worshipping your only child. Insist on a more balanced allocation of attention. Let the child know:

- "You are a wonderful part of our life, but you are not all of our life."
- "We love doing things with you, but there are also things we love doing apart from you."
- "Your wants are important, but not more so than our own."

ATTENTION GETTING AND ATTENTION GIVING

To forestall an only child from developing an only attitude, parents need to start teaching him that healthy relationships aren't meant to work just one way, for his benefit alone. They must work two ways, for the benefit of all involved. To prevent the development of the only attitude, parents must teach their child how to give attention to others as well. The name of that attention is *mutuality,* an equitable exchange of effort in relationships, practicing from an early age three important attention-giving skills upon which mutuality is based.

1. *Reciprocity* is the understanding that in all healthy relationships each party not only derives some benefit from the other's giving, but also contributes so the other enjoys some benefit in return. *Reciprocity means paying attention to the exchange of benefits in a relationship.* So the young child is told: "I want to hear what you have to say, but I want you to listen to what I have to say first."

2. *Sensitivity* is exercised by realizing that through daily intimacy, people learn a lot about each other's vulnerabilities. Out of consideration for this understanding, all parties resolve not to act in ways that will knowingly cause hurt. *Sensitivity means paying attention to each other's special needs.* So the young child is told: "Please be specially quiet this evening because loud noise just makes my headache worse."

3. *Compromise* requires that sacrifice be shared if people are to support the well-being of their relationship. *Compromise means paying attention to what one must give up to get agreement and to get along.* So the young child is told: "I'm not willing to do this all your way, only some, because I want it done partly my way, too."

Children do not come into this world immediately prepared to understand the concept of mutuality. These principles must be taught through socialization—by instruction, example, and interaction. With an only child, they must be taught in order to balance out the disproportionate amount of family attention that child is likely to receive and come to expect as his due.

Parents must teach their only child to be an attention giver or else they become complicit in raising a child who believes attention getting is what matters most. Sometimes parents believe that if they model attention giving to the only child, from their example, attention giving is what the child will learn. Unfortunately, a more common outcome from their beneficence is for the child to become an attention getter instead. As one mother of an only child wrote: "Only children who don't develop good listening skills may grow up believing that what they have to say is more important than what anyone else has to say. Even though we may enjoy listening to our only child (hard not to do when there is only one), they should hear us as well. The child who continually interrupts adults or always has to draw attention to himself is a child who isn't thinking enough about those around him."[17] If she grows up with this priority in mind, she may be "spoiled" for later relationships.

- When it comes to reciprocity, she can assume: "My needs and wants matter most."
- When it comes to sensitivity, she can assume: "My feelings should be considered first."
- When it comes to compromise, she can assume: "What's best for me is best for you."

What responsible parent wants to send an adult only child out into the world armed with these beliefs? "Give and get" is a far better preparation for an only child than "all get and no give." To this end, parents can always insist on an equitable exchange with the child, doing for her as long as she does for them. Because of the young child's dependency on them for an array of goods, services, and permissions, they should delay providing any of these unless or until the child has demonstrated adequate cooperation with them. "Balance receiving with giving" is what one psychologist advises. This means understanding that

in his position of priority, an only expects as much from you as you are willing to give. He will take for as long as it comes his way. In this respect he is no different from his 'sibling-ed' friends. The difference is that parents of onlies who have the wherewithal are prone to give to excess. If an only receives too much for too long, he will eventually demand his anticipated rewards and you will have fed the stereotype of the impatient, spoiled only child.[18]

So feel free to pay your only child plenty of attention, but make sure you also train the child to give comparable attention to others in return.

SUMMARY

Undivided parental attention is probably the most influential of all family factors shaping the only child. It continually affirms one vital fact of life for the only child: He or she is worth paying a lot of attention to.

On the strengthening side are strong self-esteem and self-definition. On the problematic side are self-importance, self-concealment, self-consciousness, becoming unduly self-centered in relationships, and the danger of developing an "only attitude"—the belief that one's welfare comes first and counts more than others in the family who are expected to subscribe to this belief.

The antidote to the only attitude is for parents to teach attention giving to balance out attention getting, and to insist on the practice of mutuality—sensitivity, reciprocity, and compromise—in relationships at home.

The antidote to excessive and invasive parental attention is for parents to respect the only child's need for privacy and to create intermittent relief from their conscientious scrutiny.

3

SENSITIVITY

A Matter of Feeling

Only children tend to develop a high degree of emotional sensitivity from the care with which parents treat them. An only child is usually given delicate parenting. It trains him to notice and respond to subtle cues in return, and to develop a carefulness and sensibility with others that can strengthen later capacities for personal intimacy as well as social tact with adults. There is often an awareness that small acts can emotionally convey and count for a lot. On the problematic side, however, is the development of an oversensitivity to the less diplomatic and more callous interactions with peers. The feelings of the only child, who is less accustomed to this impulsive rough-and-tumble, can be easily hurt. Hence the parental challenge is to be sensitive to the child without fostering oversensitivity in him.

Since they don't want to injure the precious object of all their love, parents handle him with special care. And because they care so much, whatever happens to hurt the child hurts them. In the words of one psychologist: "You're so connected to your single being that you feel every hurt, every slight . . . If you have children, you identify with their pain. You worry. But if you have a singleton, you can immerse yourself totally in her distress."[1]

Parents readily become oversolicitous with their only child because her discomfort is so painful to them. They can treat her as emotionally fragile because, in early parenthood, they feel so fragile themselves. This is where training the child in oversensitivity can begin. Experienced parents may be willing to let the infant fuss at night for a little while to see if she can settle herself down, or, when older, they may comfortably resist the child's complaints about feeling lonely and wanting to join them in bed. "Why should I have to sleep alone when you can both sleep together?" Parents of an only child may have no good answer for that, or at least not one they feel they can emotionally support. Parents of an only child often describe how they can't stand to hear her cry, how they rush in with comfort at the smallest sign of distress. Oversensitive treatment can foster an oversensitive child, but given the choice, most parents of an only child would rather be charged with being oversensitive than insensitive, an accusation very hard for them to bear. Their problem of how sensitively to treat their son or daughter does not subside as the child grows.

Come adolescence and the unwise worldly choices that can impulsively be made, parents of an only child may find it particularly hard to allow the teenager to face the consequences of his decisions. If he is picked up by the police with some sixth-grade companions for shoplifting, should the parents try to get charges dropped? The only child surely thinks so and pleads accordingly, while parents are sensitive to soothing his fears and preventing a juvenile record from compromising his future. From here on, growing-up issues can get even more challenging for sensitive parents.

They sometimes tiptoe around issues that should be directly confronted. For example, consider the high school sophomore whose parents discovered she was using drugs but didn't confront her for fear of wounding her feelings. In doing so, they failed to provide the direction she needed. To a counselor they explained, "If she's using drugs, there must be something emotionally wrong. And whatever else we do, we need to avoid making her feel worse by declaring what she doesn't want us to know. She gets so easily upset. Besides, what we're really worried about is the underlying issue beneath her use. Is it low self-esteem? Is it depression? That's our real concern." And so they allowed sensitivity to their daughter's emotional vulnerability to keep them from doing the responsible thing—bringing direct attention to her illicit substance use. They needed to help her evaluate whether or not her use was within a normal experimental range and identify the motivation for this behavior, whether for personal pleasure, from peer pressure, or from the need to self-medicate emotional pain. They needed to gather the courage to be *in*sensitive enough to her feelings to address the choice to use that she made. *"Tough love" is very hard for most parents to give their only child at any age: to speak plainly about difficult issues, to stick to unpopular demands and limits, and to allow or apply hard consequences when appropriate.*

Finally, consider an even older only child, a very sensitive, socially shy young man who has just announced to his parents his life plan. Instead of going to college after high school, he is joining the military. His choice scares and horrifies them. "Why?" they ask, filled with worries for the only child. "Don't you know how they will treat you?" "Yes," he answers. "They will order me around, I will be made to do hard things, and they won't care how I feel. They will help toughen me up, and that's what I believe I need." The young man is correct. While a great strength when it comes to intimacy and tact, sensitivity can also have a debilitating side.

TOO SENSITIVE FOR ONE'S OWN GOOD

Parental sensitivity that felt so good to the child can become too much for his own good as he grows older. His treatment by others may never quite measure up to this parental standard of care. In consequence, the only child can feel easily bruised and offended by roughness in relationships outside of family because he is unaccustomed to socially unsympathetic, indifferent, or injurious treatment.

If parents possessively keep the only child's company mostly to themselves, believing "just the three of us will have more fun," or bow to his preference for time mostly alone, they may fail to mix in sufficient group activity with peers. Already lacking sibling interaction, he is likely to miss out on the hard lessons learned from knocking around in a gang of peers, "an emotional training for life that is difficult, if not impossible, to replicate."[2]

To help make up for this lack of training at home, parents can coach their only child on how to deal with the social cruelty children commonly inflict on one another in late elementary and early middle school, when social meanness is used to protect insecurity and advance social interests. Should any of this harsh treatment come his way, the only child needs to know how not to take it personally, and how not to make it worse. If your child is feeling bad about himself after being teased on the playground, you can help him understand how the teasing is *not* about him, it's about them. Being teased doesn't mean that anything is wrong with him, but it says a lot about the teasers—they want to be mean. You can even explain to him the motivation behind the teasing, how teasers attack characteristics that they are afraid of being teased about themselves. "If he called you a loser, then that is what he doesn't want people calling him." Then you can also advise your child to ignore the teasing, laugh it off, and not encourage more by acting upset. Your coaching can reduce your child's vulnerability for feeling hurt by the normal cruelties of the early adolescent age. He may have difficulty processing normal emotional injury with peers, have a hard time getting used to it, or perhaps hold himself back to guard against it. Perhaps this is why he only allows himself to get close to a chosen few. "A pattern of a few close friends is apparent among only children."[3]

Denied this rough-and-tumble training, adult only children in significant relationships can take offense and suffer wounds from the normal jostling that multiple children in a family learn to shrug off as no big deal—just the usual bruising give-and-take of sibling life. For example, in counseling I have seen adult only children very emotionally vulnerable to experiences which their partners, who grew up with brothers and sisters, may not have cared for, but accepted and expected as how relationships sometimes are. For example:

- being treated as unimportant or less important than others,
- being left out or left behind,
- being on the losing end of an argument or competition,
- being uninformed or misinformed,
- being taken for granted or unappreciated,
- being treated unfairly or taken advantage of,
- being told what to do and not consulted or asked,
- being blamed, criticized, or found unworthy,
- being short-changed or given an unequal share,

- being let down by a broken agreement or promise,
- being teased, made fun of, or put down,
- being rejected, neglected, or ignored,
- being denied recognition for accomplishment.

From what I have seen, these can be common hot buttons for many adult only children who are more emotionally thin-skinned than those who grew up with siblings and are by comparison more thick-skinned, and less easily irritated, offended, or hurt. The adult with siblings probably didn't like this treatment either, but learned to deal with it, to recover and move on, with no carryover of hard feelings when the next irritating or hurtful act occurred. Intermittent slights that the child with siblings does not internalize, enlarge upon, or hold on to, the only child may take to heart, magnify in importance, and have a hard time letting go of.

As parents of an only child, don't treat her too sensitively for her own good. Help her put adverse experiences and events into perspective by encouraging her to understand how unwanted and hard things happen to people in relationships all the time, all their lives. Try saying something like this:

The trick to not getting your feelings hurt is understanding that you always have a *choice*. Whether to feel hurt or not to feel hurt by how someone else did or didn't act is *always* up to you. *You get to decide* how you want to feel. Nobody can cause you emotional hurt without your permission. Just because you don't like an experience doesn't mean you have to take it to heart. In fact, you can minimize its emotional impact. You can say to yourself: "Just because this isn't what I expected, like, or wanted, I'm not going to make it seem bigger than it is. I'm going to deal with it as best I can, and then I'm going to move on." You can always try on these phrases to minimize emotional impact: "Hard stuff happens to everyone," "It's not so bad," "It will work out," "I'll be okay," "Things will look up," "It's not worth getting upset about."

One way to help the child reduce his sensitivity to hurt is by reducing his sense of seriousness about himself.

TOO SERIOUS FOR ONE'S OWN GOOD

Some researchers have observed, "Let's face it—only children can be dull, too conscientious, overresponsible, lacking a sense of fun . . . Life to them is a serious business, and they are not the most relaxed people when it comes to how the family presents to the world. Remember all the 'Be perfect' messages they received—those aren't easy to ignore. Remember too how, from an early age, they felt the weight of all the responsibility."[4]

That's the equation all right: *seriousness = perfection + responsibility.* The more seriously the only child takes himself, the more emotionally sensitive he becomes to unwanted events, to mistreatment, and to reverses. To quote a wife's description of her only-child husband: "Jim is so serious all the time . . . Recently . . . I got the giggles about something extremely silly. I was helpless with laughter, but he kept telling me to pull myself together. I feel sad, really, because I know that it is only that he never learned that irresponsible stuff, like I did as the youngest in a big family."[5] However, a lot that wasn't learned in childhood can be acquired as an adult, and this includes developing a sense of humor about oneself to keep excessive seriousness at bay. For example, he could lighten up around the demand and expectation for perfection.

One strategy I've used in counseling adult only children out of their serious-mindedness is to start the loosening-up and lightening-up process by giving them an assignment. Before each session they have to have prepared a Perfect Person joke. Here's a sample:

- "How many Perfect People does it take to change a light bulb?" Answer: *Two. One to screw it in and a second to criticize how badly the job was done.*
- "Why did the Perfect Person cross the road?" Answer: *To find a better way.*
- "When two Perfect People argue, who wins?" Answer: *The one who gets to have the final word.*

Sometimes this exercise in poking fun at himself in counseling can raise a more deep-seated issue—his need to protect his own self-image. He doesn't like having fun made of himself, even if he is the one making it. Self-protective against it, when it comes to directing humor toward others, he can be quite insensitive; able to dish it out, but not necessarily to take it. Even parents of an only child, when it comes to their parenting, can be too serious for their own good. Consider the earnest couple concerned about their young daughter's fear of making small missteps, much less big mistakes. The best way to teach this only child to lighten up was for the parents to lighten up—not just with the child, but with themselves. To do this, they might consider accepting their own inevitable performance failures and lapses in responsibility with a sense of humor.

Could they address and recover from what they did or didn't do with some laughter at themselves, I asked? "Why would we laugh at something that's not funny?" they wanted to know. "Because," I explained, "the more seriously you treat minor obstacles and reverses in life, the more they will hurt. And from what you have described, at the age of twelve, your daughter is acting too sensitive for her own good." Then to give them an example of how they might act differently, I suggested: "The next time one of you forgets what you meant to do for her, after apologizing and making any amends you choose, rather than get angry at yourself, try using a little self-deprecating humor. Just smile and shake your head and confess to your child: 'I can't believe I let this slip. This comes from taking on more than I can manage. You'd think I would have learned that by trying to do too much, I end up not being able to do it all. How foolish can I get?'"

By creating a humorous perspective, you can reduce the importance of what happened, the seriousness with which it is treated, and the emotional impact that it has. It can turn bemoaning a *human failing* into acceptance of a *human foible*. As a parent, if you can laugh at yourself, you can teach your only child that invaluable skill, and he or she will have a lot to thank you for as an adult.

When it comes to emotional vulnerability, not only can the only child be too sensitive and too serious for his own good, he can also be too grown-up for his own good.

TOO GROWN-UP FOR ONE'S OWN GOOD

Most only children can't have it both ways—becoming good at acting grown-up and staying good at acting one's actual age. For example, consider the only child who at age five "couldn't get along with other kids. He didn't know how to share things, how to tell funny stories, how to fall down and laugh at himself, how to cooperate, how to stand up for himself, how to fight and make up ... [He] had learned adult skills from his parents, but he had not learned childhood skills."[6] The lesson is, don't conform your only child to living with adults to the degree he lacks the formative experiences of identifying and fitting in with peers.

To help your only child mature emotionally and reduce some emotional vulnerability as an adult, there is absolutely no substitute for providing adequate opportunities to socialize with peers, particularly with groups of peers. "Your child does need to learn how to take turns, or how to stand up for herself or when to yield center stage ... Your child is getting sibling rivalry experiences with friends."[7] It's worth repeating the four lessons that group socializing can teach the only child, lessons that can season him emotionally:

- learning how to take turns;
- standing up for oneself;
- yielding center stage;
- getting sibling rivalry experiences with friends.

The critical effect of having no siblings is not *that the only child is deprived of a big happy family and suffers from missing the good feeling companionship with other children at home. The critical effect is that the only child is deprived of a big* unhappy *family, not all the time, but enough of the time so that the ups and downs of intermittent unhappiness, with siblings particularly, are not experienced as a normal part of family life.*

For adult only children, social maturity is a mixed blessing: They grow up with a social advantage by being well prepared to negotiate their way in the adult world, but are at an emotional disadvantage in significant relationships in which they may have some emotional growing up to do. "It appears that social poise may be gained at the expense of emotional growth."[8] If part of an only child's vulnerability is her susceptibility to emotional injury in relationships, another can be having difficulty letting injury go. Socialized with kid gloves by parents, the only child may come to believe she deserves this sensitivity and consideration and may come to expect it as her due, regarding harshness from others as a betrayal of how relationships are meant to be.

HOLDING ON TO HURT

Looking back, one adult only child reflected on this tendency for holding on to hurt. "I am not very good at forgiving and forgetting... I collect 'brown stamps,' the reminders of life's injustices. When I'm crossed, taken advantage of, treated unfairly, I file the event away in my memory bank, which compounds interest daily. Later, when the appropriate key is punched into the lock, I haul it out... I'm a scorekeeper... Why? I think it's part of the legacy of the only child."[9]

If as an adult only child you are a scorekeeper, then make every effort to let this inclination go. Scorekeeping only builds a base of hard feelings that make subsequent hardships more difficult to bear, and communicates unwillingness to forgive the offender. As parents, if you see your only child prepared to end a friendship because of hurt feelings or from having a fight, encourage reconciliation by asking your child to answer five questions.

1. "If this incident had not happened, would you still want to be friends?"
2. "What about the friendship will you miss?"
3. "What would you be willing to do to help make up?"
4. "What would you need the other person to do to help make up?"
5. "What do you think you would both most enjoy doing together again?"

Some only children find it easier to cut and run when relationships with peers get hard, to retreat into the simple safety of life at home. As parents, you need to help your child accept, work through, and recover from inevitable hurts in their relationships because every time they do so strengthens them for managing relationships later on. And if you can get your only child to answer question number five, about what they would most enjoy doing together again, you can offer to help make that happen. "This weekend, I'll take you both out if you would like." What you don't want your child to do is to nurse a grudge. Because an only child has a hard time getting used to normal emotional injury in relationships, he can have an especially hard time getting over a hurt and letting it go.

It's a tendency the only child must recognize: Attach grievance to memory of hurt and you risk nursing a grudge that can grow unbridgeable later on. Rifts in important relationships can result, as one adult only child explained in counseling: "After my father had an affair, divorced my mom, and married 'the other woman,' I was never really close to him again. Instead of doing what he wanted, to get help talking stuff out between us, I held on to my anger and let divorce lose me my dad."

Dealing with hurts, children with siblings learn how to forget and forgive—to move on. For the only child, it can feel more natural to remember and resent—to hold on. Because the only child often sees no good reason for letting an emotional injury go, parents can explain to him:

- "The reason to *forgive* is to release yourself from anger and the other person from blame so you can enjoy each other's company again";
- "The reason to *forget* is to stop attaching pain to memory that takes energy and attention away from your future."

Teach your only child the twin skills of making up: the willingness to forgive and the capacity to forget—forgetting not in the sense of obliterating memory, but in ceasing to invest a memory with active pain. When it comes to his sensitivity, support the strengths of intimacy it creates in your only child and teach him to manage vulnerability so it does not get in his emotional way.

SUMMARY

The relationship between parents and the only child is typically extremely close, not just because of an exclusive attachment, but also because they are so empathetically connected. The only child learns to have a high degree of emotional sensitivity to self and to parents from their sensitivity to her. Usually, she carries this characteristic into friendships as she grows up and into significant relationships as an adult. On the up side, this fosters a carefulness and sensitivity with others than can strengthen later capacities for personal intimacy as well as social tact, an awareness of how small actions can count for a lot emotionally. On the down side, however, there are some potential difficulties that parents can help the young person forestall. For example, there can be tendencies toward being

- too sensitive for one's own good,
- too serious for one's own good,
- too grown-up for one's own good,
- too unforgiving for one's own good.

To reduce these potentialities, parents can take a number of helpful actions. They can arrange for adequate socializing with same-age children to emotionally toughen the child up in the rough and tumble of peer group play. They can help the child lighten up by cultivating a sense of humor about herself to maintain a healthy perspective. They can encourage the growth of emotional maturity to complement social maturity that develops at an early age. And they can teach the child to let go of hard feelings arising from occasional slights and affronts that are a normal part of any friendship. It's a delicate job, but what parents need to do is affirm the young person's capacity for sensitivity while moderating her vulnerability to emotional injury, particularly in childhood friendships and adult relationships that matter.

4

CONSTANCY

A Matter of Order

Only children can be constant during times of change—keeping commitments, staying organized, sticking to a schedule. They are not easily thrown off course after having made a plan or established a routine. Constancy gives them stability. A lot of what appears to be their resistance to change is actually investment in keeping conditions the same. On the problematic side, however, they usually don't welcome change they have not initiated. Making last-minute alterations for the sake of opportunity, variety, or spontaneity is usually not to their liking. Being flexible and adjusting to unexpected or unwanted change can be very hard for them to do because it feels out of their control.

In fact, the only child can feel easily overwhelmed by change, seeing it as a sign of chaos, experiencing it as an "inability to put order into life."[1] Even modest deviation from the expected can feel out of control, as one adult child reported of her need to minimize unanticipated change. "I need to be in control. Not necessarily in charge, but I do need to be in control of things I do . . . I like to plan, to know in advance. I don't like people dropping in at two minutes' notice. I'm sociable, but it has to be in my context."[2] Familiar order and continuity contribute to the constancy of life experience that many only children seem to want.

Why this preference for constancy over change? Think about the contrast between firstborns and laterborns that research has supported and that bears on the only child. Singletons "are typically closer to firstborns on openness to experience. The reason is that only children, like other firstborns, tend to identify with parents and authority."[3] This identification with parental authority causes the only child to embrace the way parents believe, do things, and order and operate family life. The firstborn and only child is more likely to embrace the status quo and defend it, in contrast to laterborns, who claim more freedom of diversity and so are more to the experience of change. Laterborns identify with parents less. Much research supports the view that "laterborns should score higher than firstborns on Openness to Experience, a dimension that is associated with being unconventional, adventurous, and rebellious. This prediction stems from the lesser identification that laterborns have with parents . . . Laterborns are more inclined than firstborns to question authority and to resist pressure to conform to a consensus. Firstborns, in contrast, tend to endorse conventional morality. Studies also reveal that laterborns are more risk orientated than firstborns."[4] Firstborns and only children tend to be more conservative, more conventional, and more reluctant to change the established order in life than laterborns.

Also, keep in mind the only child's sensitivity (see previous chapter). "The one characteristic exhibited most consistently by sensitive children of all ages is difficulty adapting to change. The unpredictability of new situations increases the sensitive child's sense of personal vulnerability and fear of possible danger. Anxious children cope much better when the predictability of daily life is increased."[5]

Of course, the question is what comes first? Is it that the only child desires predictability because he is sensitive or that his parents foster a sense of vulnerability by being too protective? The answer is, both factors are in play in *the only child's preference for constancy over change.* Among only children who are a product of parental disunion, does divorce cause them to be more amenable to change? My observation is that it usually does not. Parental divorce is so painful that it tends to harden the child against change, rather than make them more welcoming of it, because of "the multiple losses [this] change creates."[6]

The constancy on which the only child is most reliant is the stability of family functioning that parents carefully create and conscientiously maintain. They do so to meet their own needs for control and to provide the child with security. The parental lifestyle at home establishes an ambiance that the only child strives to respect by fitting into the practices they live by, by going along with the conditions they set, and by committing to the values and traditions they hold dear. Why is the only child so agreeable?

- Parental terms are usually tailored to the child's comforts, so she has little desire to change what works so well and feels so good.
- The child strongly imitates and identifies with his parents because they are the sole home companions he has, encouraging conformity with them.
- Opposition to parental stands risks arousing their disapproval and endangering their support, both of which feel scary.

Although parents credit themselves with having ample sway over the only child, at least until the boy or girl's adolescence, they actually *underestimate* the influence that their attachment, approval, and power of example commands.

THE COSTS OF CONSTANCY

To keep their only child secure, parents strive for family constancy in the form of establishing and maintaining order, sameness, continuity, tradition, routines, predictability, and familiarity. And when a major change is chosen, as in a geographic move, or required, as in a change of schools, parents give a lot of thought to preparation and planning to help the child anticipate adjustments that will need to be made. To the degree that parents can pave the way to change with careful planning for their child, they do so.

The outcome of their constancy and care with making changes can be feeling comfort now at the expense of discomfort later. Just as extremely sensitive parents can nurture an extremely anxious child (see chapter 16), *an extremely constant upbringing can produce a child who is very intolerant of change.* He can be prone to worry and other emotional upset when change occurs, particularly disruptive change that has or can have a negative impact on his life. (Disruptive change is what happens when events are neither expected nor desired.) In contrast, many children grow up comfortable with change.

Those raised in military families, for example, often become extremely skilled at making changes, even welcoming the challenge of moving every two years. They get used to pulling up stakes, letting go old friends, leaving what is familiar, facing uncertainty, tolerating confusion, adjusting to different demands, fitting into a strange circumstance, making new social connections, exploiting new possibilities, and getting to experience strange surroundings. They find change exciting and interesting, and even feel bored when life proceeds too much the same. Needless to say, this welcoming attitude and adaptability to change is usually *not* characteristic of most only children, who may view it primarily as a losing and scary proposition and resist it on that account.

DELAYING ADOLESCENT CHANGE

Investment in familiarity can cause the child to cling to constancy and avoid or resist change. It is this resistance that often delays the social changes of adolescence for many only children, who may not start this pushing for more independence until as late as early high school, when by the beginning of middle school most other children are already well under way.[7] Only children want to act older, but they don't want to grow up. This delay by only children seems motivated by

- benefits they feel they have to lose by letting childhood go,
- the uncertainty and insecurity the next phase of growing up creates,
- parental disapproval and loneliness that asserting more independence can bring.

For all children, the process of adolescence requires courage because separating from parents and expressing new individuality takes daring to do. But for the only child, so firmly anchored in family comfort and tradition, this process of change, with its loss of the familiar and fear of the unknown, can be scariest of all. By family circumstance, *the only child is more accustomed to constancy than to change.*

By adulthood, some only children have become orderly to the point that they are wed to a routine. They like things the way they are. The comfort of constancy is what they want, not change. If something is not on the schedule or on the list, if it's disruptive of plans, if it spontaneously arises or is otherwise out of order, the adult only child often prefers that it not be done. So what contributes to this intolerance for change?

CONSTANCY FROM UNMODIFIED ATTACHMENT

The primary adjustment that the only child and the parents who limited the family to a single child are *not* given an opportunity to make is the integration of another child into the family. Reorganization of family life around a second child not only creates additional demands on the parents, but deeply compromises them as well. With a second child they can never again give as much of themselves as they did to child number one, and they cannot give as much of themselves to the second child as they once did to the first. On both counts they may feel guilty as charged. As for the only child, family life will never be the same, as one six-year-old charged his parents in counseling.

"Why did you want to have more than me?" she asked indignantly.

"Because," they explained, "you've been so wonderful, we wanted another."

"If I'm so wonderful," argued the child, "then why wasn't I enough?"

It's hard for parents to comprehend the massive change that their only, now oldest, child is growing through. Preoccupied with new family responsibilities, it's hard for them to register her sense of loss.

- *Disappointment:* feeling insufficient to satisfy all parental wants.
- *Displacement:* feeling moved off center stage to make room for another player.
- *Demotion:* feeling a loss of status from being adult companion to becoming another child.
- *Dethronement:* feeling a loss of power from no longer ruling the family roost.

- *Dejection:* feeling sadness over the loss of exclusive privileges conferred by being an only child.
- *Detachment:* feeling less close to parents now that a rival has claimed their affections.

Does this mean that having a second child is so painful to the first that parents should just stick to one? No. But they need to understand that changes caused by the arrival of a brother or sister demand a massive and ongoing adjustment. They bring long-lasting companionship, competition, comparison, and conflict into the only child's life where there was none before.

To appreciate the power of this change, think of how most only children, at least by adolescence, do *not* want this change to happen. As has been noted, many "only children who are comfortable with themselves tend to look upon their status as natural, even ordained . . . not aware of wanting a brother or sister. [Reported one:] 'It never occurred to me that my parents would want anyone else . . . My guess is that it never occurred to me that they would dare have anyone but me' . . . 'When I was growing up, I didn't know a brother or sister who had a kind word to say about a sibling. I never saw that I was missing anything except a headache or an upset stomach.'"[8]

I believe a major reason why so many only children find the changing nature of life so challenging and are so needful of control during changing times is because they never had to make the primal and continuing adjustment to family change caused by the arrival of another child. To this bias toward constancy, there is one other that is rooted in the parents, not the only child.

CONSTANCY FROM INVESTMENT IN THE STATUS QUO

As described by the demographic trends described in chapter 1, the longer people wait to start a family, the fewer children they tend to have, and the older the parents are when they begin. Being older can be a significant factor in the parental attitudes toward change with which the only child is raised. As researchers have observed, "A very large

number of only children are born after their parents are 30 . . . The difference in attitudes between generations, especially in this era of rapid
change, increases as the differential between parent and child increases.
Older parents are likely to be set in their ways, to be overprotective,
and unsympathetic. Age is conservative, youth is experimental."[9]

Older parents of an only child are often

- invested in the social and economic position they have established,
- firmly set in their beliefs about how life should be conducted,
- protective of what they have and what they want carried on,
- less tolerant of diversity between them and their adolescent.

This conservative attitude toward change is often part of the
parental mind-set with which the only child identifies. She is more
likely to want to carry on what parents represent than to challenge or
change it for herself, when grown up; in effect, the only child does not
usually fall far from the parental tree. Most adult only children I have
had in counseling would agree with this statement: "I turned out
more similar to my parents than different." This similarity between
them often strengthens their friendship during the child's adult years
by providing a common bond based on shared values and enjoyments.

On the problematic side, however, when it comes to continuing
or modifying tradition, the only child sometimes tends to be reac-
tionary.[10] The only child is usually supportive of the established order
that was learned at home and is resistant to personal and family
change. In the conduct and arrangement of his life, personal order has
a very high value. According to one only-child researcher, "Onlies
don't like it if somebody messes up their long and often detailed lists.
Because Onlies are so organized, it drives them even further over the
edge when they are interrupted. Onlies expect order. They demand it.
They need it. Once they get things organized, they expect things to
stay that way."[11]

The parental need for household order often comes into play. In
the only-child home, peace and quiet tend to trump what the addition of siblings can provide—moments of riotous disorder created by

the combustion of spontaneous outbursts of unhappiness or pleasure. Although adult only children will sometimes regret missing these unexpected interactions, as grown-ups they seem to be more inclined to desire order, predictability, and calm, partly from the absence of siblings and partly because that is what the parents preferred. In the two-parent household, the only child is outnumbered and is expected to fit into the living arrangement that works for them.

As a consequence of this reliance on order, he isn't likely to welcome more change than is required, and is often resistant to that. Add to this reluctance his being trained by parents to *plan* for change. By usually choosing to have a single child and carefully deciding how to raise the child, parents contribute to the child's preference for order over change. "One characteristic of parents of a single child that is consistently noted by researchers is *planning:* Parents of an only child tend not to be 'rushers into things.'"[12]

Parents of only children tend to have a strong commitment to planned child raising, controlling for the growth they want, preventing what they do not want, shaping a child who is more reliant on these controls than open to the freedom that permits exploratory and spontaneous change. Given this preference for constancy, what he needs is parental help in learning to manage change because this revolutionary process will keep *upsetting* and *resetting* the order of his experience as long as he lives.

HELPING YOUR CHILD COPE WITH CHANGE

To begin this education, parents can explain it in terms the child can identify and understand.

What is change? They can begin with a working definition: *Change is that process that takes us from an old to a new, from the same to a different, from a familiar to a strange, from a known to an unknown situation, condition, or relationship.* They can then break down the process operationally into four basic kinds of events that always signify that change is occurring:

- whenever something *starts* happening,
- whenever something *stops* happening,

- whenever something *increases,*
- whenever something *decreases.*

A geographic move provides a good illustration of how parents can help their only child learn to cope with significant life change, for it is usually a mixture of all four kinds of change in one. Consider how parents might proceed with an only child of late elementary school age who is extremely upset about being uprooted to live in another state, all for the sake of one parent's new job. "It will all be different! There's nothing I can do!" the child protests upon receiving the news, seeing the change in threatening terms—as a complete loss of the familiar, and herself as a victim of circumstance in which she has no power of choice. To defuse this emotional response, parents must exercise their *predictive responsibility*—helping their child learn how to anticipate likely ways the change may realistically alter her life. "If we can predict, then we can prepare," they can explain.

Then, using the framework of the four kinds of changes, they can sit down and brainstorm all the hard specifics that will start, stop, increase, and decrease with the move.

- If the child says, "I will have to *start* making new friends," parents can reply, "We can help you do that by meeting other parents and inviting their children to come over."
- If the child says, "I will *stop* seeing my old friends," parents can reply, "We can help you keep up long-distance contact with visits and communication."
- If the child says, "I will have to catch up on my math," parents can reply, "And we'll help tutor you to *increase* your skills."
- If the child says, "I'm going to have less time with you because of your new job," a parent can reply, "You and I will use weekends to make up for any *decrease* in time together during the week."

The message parents want to give the child is that while change always creates challenges, many can be anticipated and prepared for. But what about the unanticipated changes? If preparing your only child to manage expected change is one parental responsibility, training her to get used to unexpected change is another. *Flexibility* and *adaptability* are skills she will need when what was sure becomes uncertain or untrue, as often happens in life when conditions shift, plans are upset, or agreements are broken.

For most abilities that parents nurture in their child, some degree of inability is created. Hence the only child, who is so well secured by the clarity of parental expectations, consistency of family routines, reliability of parental commitments, and sense of personal control, can come to count on this vital support in a rigid way:

- "But you never told me this might happen; this isn't fair!" (violated expectations);
- "But we've always done it this way; I don't want to change!" (violated household routine);
- "But you promised; you can't go back on your word!" (violated parental commitment);
- "But I don't want to do it your way; I want to do it my way!" (violated personal control).

In their desire to create security at home, parents may inadvertently reduce an only child's capacity to deal with the normal chaos of life over which no one has control. Parents have to teach that flexibility and adaptability are as important to security as constancy, and they can be learned. How?

Within the sheltered social reality of the family,

- Parents can teach flexibility and adaptability by approaching some experiences free of expectations.

  Child: "What will it be like when we get there? What will we do?"

  Parent: "I don't know exactly. We'll just have to see what it's like and then figure out what we want to do."

- Parents can treat routines themselves as partly flexible.

  Child: "Why aren't you going to read me a bedtime story tonight?"

Parent: "Because I'm tired and really need to get to bed myself. Maybe there's a way for you to do a bedtime story for
yourself instead."

- Parents can treat their promises as what they want and mean
to do, but must be flexible when these commitments cannot
be met.

Child: "But you said we could! You did!"
Parent: "I meant the promise when I made it, but that was before everyone got sick. I still want to keep that promise,
but now we'll have to do it another time."

- Parents can treat control of decision making as flexible in relationships, shifting back and forth as people take turns.

Child: "I want to decide like I did before!"
Parent: "Sometimes it's important to let others decide, so this
time we're going to choose instead."

The parental goal needs to be teaching *resilience:* when circumstances change, the only child should have the confidence and skills to
make effective changes in response.

LOOSENING UP

Sheltering the only child with constancy at home may set her up for
difficulty in adjusting to changes in the outside world, where flexibility
and adaptability are necessary for healthy survival. So loosen your child
up. Just because being relaxed around change is not your parental way
does not mean that your child cannot learn more flexibility by spending time with other families or trusted adults who are more spontaneous, improvisational, exploratory, spur-of-the-moment decision
makers than you. For example, while you may take your only child on
carefully designed and precisely scheduled trips, part of the fun of traveling with more fluid people is encountering and adapting to the surprising and the unexpected. So when your child takes off on an outing
with them, she gets to experience a very different attitude toward

change. In such company, your child can learn to follow curiosity, seek adventure, welcome surprise, and explore unanticipated opportunities.

This need for constancy is often evident in the adult only child who relies on calculating, list making, scheduling, organizing, and planning to minimize and manage change. As some observers have noted, "When an Only Child adult has decided on a schedule of activities, for example, he or she expects to follow it to the letter. There's no way this person is going to do number three on the list before the two items preceding it have been completed."[13]

The need of the adult only child to proceed strictly according to plan can strike her partner as excessive. So in counseling, the partner pleads: "Why do last-minute changes upset you so much? Why do you throw up your hands as if you're being threatened or betrayed? If I want to change my mind at the last minute, why shouldn't I? Why can't you just go with the flow? Change isn't some kind of problem. It's how life is!"

Then the following dialogue unfolds.

> Adult only child: "You can't change your mind, not after we've already made plans!"
>
> Partner: "Oh come on, plans are made to be broken if they don't feel good when the time comes or something better comes along."
>
> Adult only child: "There's no point in making a plan if you're not going to stick to it! Plans are made so we know what we are going to do."
>
> Partner: "But I don't like always knowing what I'm going to do. I like to be surprised. Besides, a plan isn't some kind of promise that has to be kept. It's just a possibility."
>
> Adult only child: "Not to me it isn't. If we go to the trouble of scheduling something, then that's what needs to happen."
>
> Partner: "I can't live with that kind of inflexibility."
>
> Adult only child: "And I can't be switching plans every time you change your mind!"
>
> Partner: "You can if you stop making so many plans!"

Once in a significant relationship, the adult only child may have some loosening up to do with a partner who complains about his rigid behavior and insistence on following a strict agenda in life. Fortunately, loosening up can be learned through practice by letting go and relaxing controls, trusting to one's own resilience, and treating change not just as a threat to the established order, but as a bearer of opportunity as well.

SUMMARY

The only child tends to be more accustomed to constancy than to change because

- attachment to parents and to the routine of family functioning are spared adjustment to an additional child;
- parents strive to provide security by creating order and consistency;
- an only child tends to have older parents who are more settled in their ways and invested in preserving what they value.

In consequence, the only child may lack the flexibility and adaptability needed to cope with the relative chaos of life once he leaves the shelter of his parents' protective care. Then he may feel nervous, get uptight, or even throw up his hands when the expected does not materialize or when the unexpected does. To keep life safely in order, he may be prone to extreme control taking—given to careful planning, organizing, scheduling, and list making to feel secure. All else being equal, the adult only child is more inclined to choose constancy over variety, and continuity over change.

As for parents of an adolescent only child, they usually have an only child who prefers predictability to surprise, who is more methodical and less impulsive than peers with siblings, inclined to stick to plans and promises once made.

5

FRIENDSHIP

A Matter of Loyalty

Only children tend make good friends. That is, only children tend to be very selective in the friends they choose, carefully screening them for compatibility, giving loyalty and commitment and receiving them in return. They value lasting relationships over casual acquaintances and so are more interested in having a small circle of friends than in being social butterflies. On the problematic side, however, the quality of adult friendship they enjoy with parents can be an ill-fitting model for same-age peers. It can be hard for them to find friends because they act socially older and out of step when interacting with many peers. When they are uncomfortable in peer groups, they may keep themselves at a certain social distance: they are not usually joiners, often preferring to spend time alone.

According to stereotypes, an only child is at a disadvantage when forming same-age friendships. Why? Three explanations are commonly given:

- Often left to himself, the only child is solitary from spending *time alone*.
- The only child relies on *parents for primary companionship*.
- The only child *lacks siblings* with whom to play and practice getting along.

In fact, none of these three factors of only-child life precludes making friends, but each does have a bearing on how friendships are often made. Consider how each influence can be felt.

TIME ALONE

Here's a riddle: How do you grow up alone and not be lonely? The answer for most only children is that you learn to be your own companion. You develop ways to be by yourself that are rewarding, pursuing interests and developing skills that parents can and should support. According to one observer,

> Most people who are not only children think of only children as lonely. But there is a big difference between being alone and being lonely. "Lonely" is supposed to mean "sad for the lack of companionship"... Being alone does not necessarily mean being sad. Being alone is simply not having anyone around, and it can be great. Alone times are time to grow, to dream, to get to know yourself... Everyone should learn to love quiet and make an effort to be alone sometimes. Everybody needs privacy... Only children usually have all the privacy they need, since there are no brothers and sisters to be pests... Studies show that many only children grow up to use their creativity... Because of the alone time as a child, these children have been able to stimulate their creativity.[1]

The only child can make up much entertainment, including the company of imaginary friends. "You make up games, you make up imaginary friends. You spend a lot of time alone out of necessity. Instead of talking to someone, you talk to yourself and think about things. That's why I'd say I'm a more introspective person and have a much wider imagination."[2] As this only child testifies, time alone is often imagination time.

It has been observed how this capacity for fantasy friendship can play out in the only child's adult life. "This imaginary friend business turns into serious work as Onlies grow up and turn into Only Child adults. Onlies never seem to let go of their love for this imaginary section of life...Onlies don't wash their cars. They give them baths. They think the cars will feel bad if they were dirty—and would feel worse if they were sold...These types of attachments do not just extend to cars...Onlies love their things and love to be at home, alone, surrounded by them."[3] Emotional investment in the imagined vitality of possessions can create an unusual sense of attachment to personal objects. "Things" can have special value for the only child, creating a kind of beloved company.

Time alone, far from being painful, becomes rewarding because the only child is establishing a bond of lasting benefit—a primary friendship with himself. This bond creates a foundation of self-sufficiency that contributes to the only child's independence, an enjoyment of solitude, and an affirmative relationship to himself. Consider what a few only children have to say in witness to this:

- "I was frequently left to my own devices and became a pro at entertaining myself, gaining a tremendous sense of independence early on."[4]
- "I like myself and, because I do, I'm able to like other people too."[5]
- "I belong to a group of people who don't want to be part of a group."[6]
- "Like nearly every other only child I've ever met, I prefer to be alone."[7]
- "I have a very small circle of friends. I like to be by myself a lot."[8]

Someone who is well connected to herself tends to connect well with others because she has confidence in the person she is and what she has to offer. She is not in need of someone else to validate her worth or complete her sense of definition. She is not desperate for companionship with peers because she is already well attached to herself and to her parents. Consequently, *she can afford to be selective in the friendships she makes, and she usually is.*

The only child's capacity to be comfortable with herself, by herself, creates enormous social stability during the early and mid adolescent period (roughly ages nine to fifteen) when peer pressure can be the undoing of so many young people who are dependent on friends for self definition and self-esteem. During these years, that can be so painfully insecure for others, the only child likes herself well enough, and likes being by herself well enough, that she has no need to sacrifice her self and conform socially in order to belong or to follow others. In fact, others often see the only child as a kind of leader and will follow her. *Secure aloneness creates social independence.* In addition to being well connected to parents and very comfortable at forming good relationships with teachers, only children can rely on companionships with adults to offset the overwhelming need for peer attachment at this age. *Attachment to adults reduces undue reliance on peers.*

But parents of only children are prone to worry. Does time alone create a child who is lonely? Best to put this concern to rest. According to one expert, "Many only children, then, tend to enjoy 'loner'-type activities. But according to much research, the majority of them don't *feel lonely*... and researchers concluded 'that the lack of siblings during childhood does not necessarily lead to chronic loneliness in young adulthood.'"[9]

One psychologist gives this sound advice: "The capacity to entertain oneself serves a person well in later life. Everyone has periods of time in which they are without other people. It is more enjoyable when that time alone is productive. It's a positive feeling to know how to be by yourself without having to run, without having to be busy every minute. There is a strong tendency on the part of parents to fear that their child is lonesome and, hence, deprived. When your only child is happily occupied with an endeavor, view his contentment as a plus. Don't feel compelled to be his playmate or to find him one."[10] Most only children grow up independent and personally resourceful from being so alone. And they can be prone to "friend fatigue." They like having friends over, but they can grow weary of this companionship and miss time with no one around.

ARE SIBLINGS MISSED?

Despite such good counsel, the only child's time alone and the lack of sibling companionship can often trouble parents; they may feel pangs of guilt when their preadolescent child fondly wishes for a younger brother or sister. Are siblings missed? Yes and no. They are *romanti-*

cally missed as idealized companions, but they are not *realistically missed* as actual competitors. One parent brought this distinction home to his nine-year-old son, who was wistfully wondering what he had missed by not having a younger brother. "I'll tell you part of what you missed," the dad explained. "You see all this," and the man gestured to belongings in the boy's room. "Well, think of it this way. If you had a younger brother, you would do without about half of everything here because of what we would be giving him."

On the cusp of entering that more selfish age of adolescence, the boy was able to use this explanation to appreciate one realistic benefit of being an only. Perhaps he moderated the romantic longing for an idealized younger brother who would be a tagalong companion when no better friend could be found. Missing a sibling is much more commonly expressed in childhood (up to about age nine) than in adolescence when the teenager not only grows more self-preoccupied, but also hears complaints from friends about their siblings. No matter how beloved, a younger sibling can be a pest, an older one can be bossy, and both can be combatants and competitors in family life. In addition, although he may enjoy the rich complexity of a friend's multichild family life, the only child usually likes to return home to the order, peace, and quiet of his simpler, more manageable situation.

So why the complaints about not having siblings? Consider this opinion:

> The only child who complains bitterly about not having siblings, who talks often about feeling cheated or short-changed, tends not to speak positively about the relationship with the parents. This suggests to me that these only children in reality may be criticizing their parents but, because they aren't doing this head on, focus their criticism on lack of siblings instead. It is rare for me to meet an only child who speaks lovingly of his relationship with his parents and who simultaneously expresses resentment over not having brothers and sisters. I think it may come down to this: All parents load a lot of stuff on their children, but especially on the only child. If most of it is good stuff, the child isn't eager to share it with anybody else. But if most of it is bad, the child, quite understandably, would like to have siblings who could shoulder some of the burden.[11]

I agree. The better the relationship with parents feels, the less the only child, particularly come adolescence, is going to want to share family life with a sibling, the more content she is likely to feel about being alone or in the company of a few very well chosen friends.

This legacy of learning to enjoy time alone carries into the only child's adult life. Adult only children will describe themselves as having a solitary streak. Any partner to whom they commit must accept this solitary streak as an ingrained characteristic.

PARENTS FOR PRIMARY COMPANIONSHIP

Particularly when younger, but often extending through adolescence, the only child's parent remains a friend. "Parents of only children, especially single parents, almost can't help this tendency to turn the child into a peer companion."[12] Parents have a significant standing as friends in the only child's world. "The friendship of parents is an advantage of being an only child. There is more time for being together and more opportunities for parents to know and understand their lone offspring."[13] There is a general principle of intimacy between parents and children that supports this observation. A difficulty in having multiple children is "the demands of the many preventing the intimacy among the few."[14] From inclusion in her parental world, the only child develops a kind of intimate friendship with parents that children growing up with siblings often lack. As one only child reported, this friendship with parents is a highly valued part of growing up. "I felt I was better friends with my parents than most children are. I was treated as an equal as well as a child."[15]

This quality of friendship between parents and an only child is less commonly experienced in families where parents have multiple children to manage, in which children spend more time focused on each other. In multiple child families, where the distinction between parent and child is more distinctly drawn, where "the kids" have each other as companions, children and parents know each other less intimately well. From the only child's intimacy with parents, two other favorable outcomes occur.

First, friendship with parents in childhood, which often continues unbroken by much rebellion during the adolescent years, sets a *standard for friendship* with peers that causes the only child to be selective in choosing friendships that are comparably serious, stable, deeply satisfying, and likely to last. Often chosen is another only child who is similarly inclined, or at least a companion who is more autonomous and mature. I have repeatedly seen parents in counseling who are concerned with how their high school–age daughter bypasses casual dating to become romantically involved with a man several years her senior. "Why?" the parents want to know, "does our daughter want to get serious, and why with someone so much older?" The answer is that their only-child daughter makes this choice because she is interested in

- a serious relationship, not a casual one;
- a secure relationship, not an undependable one;
- a man whose maturity makes him a more fitting companion.

As for only-child boys in late adolescence, they are often more interested in having enjoyable and meaningful *relationships* with girls then pursuing them for one-night stands.

And second, sustained companionship with parents creates a platform of commonality on which ongoing adult friendship is often built. They enjoy each other's grown-up company partly because by then there is so much communal experience and similarity of enjoyment that they have come to share. Good friends growing up, they remain good friends as adults.

Of course, like everything else, the gift of good friendship with parents can have a secondary effect when it substitutes for making same-age friends, when it places the adultlike child out of social step with peers, and when parents come to treat that friendship possessively. Only children may need parental encouragement and instruction to pursue peer friendships early on. If an only child is to have friends, parents must be willing to share the child's friendship with others and not monopolize the child's company. Hence there is this sound advice:

Possessive parents can end up losing the son or daughter they were so anxious to keep to themselves. Emotional independence allows for both intimacy and separateness. A possessive relationship be-comes controlling and engulfing and there is a definite lack of re-spect for the child's separate identity. This is an unhealthy state of affairs and may lead to the child being unable to form other rela-tionships now and in the future...Parents should be wary of a child becoming inappropriately old for her age. This may happen if...the child spends too much time in adult company and not enough with children of her own age. A child who behaves too old for her age may find herself isolated from peers either from their choice or because she finds them too immature.[16]

One only child testifies to this effect. "I grew up too fast. I did not feel part of my peer group until I went to college. Everyone told me my friends would catch up, but you are who you are at the time. As a child, I was much more comfortable with older people. I would not want my child to feel as much as an outsider as I did by being adult too young."[17]

To make up for too much adult company from lack of siblings, parents need to encourage and arrange for adequate contact with same-age friends.

LACK OF SIBLINGS

From becoming well attached to herself by spending valued time alone, and from becoming well attached to parents from companion-ship and fitting in with them, the only child can make good friends, assuming she is willing to put up with the social discomfort and effort it takes. Typically the only child chooses carefully, not casually, weigh-ing such questions as:

- "Will the person and I have enough in common?"
- "Will the person offer serious friendship of a lasting kind?"
- "Will my parents approve the person whom I choose?"

From what I have seen, it's not in most only children to "run with a gang of kids" while growing up. They

- lack crowd comfort,

- bring social selectivity to choosing friendships,
- prefer serious friendships to casual acquaintances,
- feel somewhat out of social step with many of their peers.

As recently observed, "Only children may have a smaller social circle than other kids, but they do have just as many close friends."[18] One writer about only children explains it this way: "Children with siblings tend to get to know their brother's or sister's friends on a more informal, relaxed basis and so broaden their circle of acquaintances; an only child lacking these, may tend to be more intense and perhaps a little exclusive in friendships."[19] Parents can help broaden the child's circle by encouraging companionship with cousins and with children of close parental friends.

Why is the only child so selective about making friends? Why is there this concern for finding a friend with enough compatibility and commonality to build a serious friendship of a lasting kind? I believe the absence of siblings, and the desire to create some siblinglike friendship, is what is at issue here.

COMPENSATION

Sometimes an only child will marry a partner with many siblings, partly from the desire to gain the larger family he didn't have. At these gatherings, however, personal discomfort can cloud the childhood dream. As one journalist described, "While many only children look forward to acquiring more family, sometimes large numbers of new relatives can be overwhelming... 'At holidays when everyone is together [one adult only child confessed], I find I just want to get away. Everybody's talking, but nobody's listening. I just want to retreat somewhere and take a walk.'"[20] It is a sad irony when this experience occurs, the adult only child finally getting what he dreamed about only to discover he has a limited tolerance for the boisterous family he thought he had missed.

One adult only child described her need for compensation for a lack of siblings this way: "I clung to my girlfriends. I was always crossing some unspoken line with them, too, entering into relationships that were too close, too *intimate*... As a result, there was an odd friction in the relationships, an unspoken tension about how close we should be. I wanted something permanent, forever. They had that with siblings at home...I had been trying unsuccessfully to make friends into family...I was an only child and this was how only children made siblings...The more I looked at it, the more I had to acknowledge...that while I often referred to my dear friends as my family, they often referred to me as their dear, beloved friend."[21] As another adult only child writes: "I have a particular chemistry with others who want to make their friends their family."[22] Maybe this is why many only children tend to make only-child friends.

Does a lack of siblings bear on the importance of friendship for the only child? A couple of writers think so. "In establishing friendships, only children sometimes adopt that long-lost brother or sister.. .We tend to focus more attention on our friends. We don't feel that blood is necessarily thicker than water."[23] Or as another puts it: "Many only children feel they are missing something by not having brothers or sisters. They feel as if there is an empty spot that needs to be filled. So, they pick someone to be a substitute brother or sister."[24]

What an only child ends up missing through a lack of siblings is the *permanency* of relationship that kinship confers. When parents die, there are no other children with whom to share a common origin and history, with whom to come together and recall memories, and on whom, whether you see or like each other much, to make a family claim. This sense of permanency is what the only child misses, and what she often tries to reconstitute with friends. No wonder she is motivated to make serious friendships of a lasting kind. *A close friend is often partly a sibling in disguise.*

SUMMARY

The only child is shaped for friendship by two family circumstances:

- By spending and playing a lot of time alone.
- By having parents (not siblings) as primary companions in the home.

Time alone yields a capacity to enjoy one's own company, to get to know and develop one's self—one's skills and interests and one's imaginative side. Time with parents accustoms the child to older, more mature companions and encourages similarity to parents through inclusion in their world. By conforming to their older interests, wants, and ways, the child is placed somewhat out of social step with same-age peers.

Contrary to the stereotype, the only child is not more lonely than children with siblings, nor is she less capable of making friends. In fact, the capacity to be a satisfying companion to oneself and to one's parents provides confidence when it comes to making friends, which the only child does selectively and with care, usually choosing others who are similarly selective, serious, often imaginative, and mature. Able to be socially outgoing, the only child is particular about who she allows to get close.

Parents may need to refrain from acting socially possessive of their child ("The three of us can have more fun just by ourselves") and share the child's company ("Why don't you invite a friend along?"). They may also have to encourage and instruct the child about entering the peer group fray since he is not used to those rough-and-tumble ways. And they should not expect to have a child who runs with the crowd, but rather someone who prefers a smaller social circle of like-minded friends. As for adult only children, they need to respect their solitary side and the desire for a few close friendships of a serious and lasting kind.

6

WILLFULNESS

A Matter of Control

Willfulness empowers the only child in a host of strengthening ways—from speaking up about what she wants to dedicating effort to reach her goals to the stubborn determination to stick to her values no matter what others may think. The only child is not weak-willed—having no firm opinions, prone to giving up, and easily swayed by peer pressure. The willfulness of the only child contributes much to the individuality she claims. On the problematic side, however, when she wants something very much, she often believes she *should* get it, and if what is desired is delayed or denied, she can get very angry. Come adolescence, increased urgency for more independence can create an even stronger-willed teenager than parents knew as a child, one who will battle them hard around limits to her freedom that they are duty bound to set.

Before we can appreciate why only children tend to be strong-willed, it helps to understand what willfulness is. I define "willfulness" as "a person's power of self-determination to direct, to persist, and to prevail."[1] A willful child is *not* a pushover to parents. "In willful children, where there's a will there's a *want*, so they can act very *intense*. Where there's a will there's a *won't*, so they can act very *stubborn*. Where there's a will there's a *why*, so they can act very *challenging*. Where there's a will there's a *win*, so they can act very *combative*. Where there's a will, there's a *when*, so they can act very *impatient*. And where there's a will there's a *whose*, so they can act very *possessive*.

Willfulness takes a variety of common forms, and parents must be ready to contend with them all."[2]

What separates willful children from those who are not is how they manage *not* getting what they want. When children who are not generally willful are denied what they want, they may feel sad, shrug off the disappointment, and then go on to something else. Willful children, however, tend to have a different response: *telltale anger.*

The emotional hallmark of the willful child is getting angry when he doesn't get what he wants. Why? Because he makes a *conditional shift.* His intense desire turns his aspiration into an imperative, and an imperative into a condition. "I want to have" turns into "I must have" turns into "I *should* have," and the result is anger when the willful child is denied what he now feels entitled to: "If I want it, then I should get it!" "If I don't want to do it, I shouldn't have to!"

The parent's job is to help the willful child learn to disconnect "should" from "want," to let go of the conditional view through which he sees the situation. So the parent says something like this: "I know when you want something very much it feels like you should be allowed to get it, but life isn't like that. Wanting something very much doesn't mean we should get it. Wanting just means there's something we'd like to have or do, and maybe we'll get some of it, and maybe we won't. And if we don't, we'll still be okay."

Although endowed human nature can certainly contribute to a child's willfulness—some infants are extremely demanding and easily frustrated from birth while others are constitutionally placid and patient—I believe parental nurture plays a more influential role, particularly when it comes to an only child. In the words of one adult only child looking back: "Because I was an only child, I had an incredible strength regarding what I did and didn't want to do."[3] Many only children would say the same.

Why does the only child usually become so willful? Consider four family dynamics that can encourage this characteristic to occur.

- The temptation for *parental indulgence.*
- The conferring of *adult-like standing.*

- The example of *strong-willed parents.*
- The nurturing of *strong individuality.*

Start with the first source of willfulness in the only child.

PARENTAL INDULGENCE

Relative to what they can *afford,* parents are usually very giving to their only child. Relative to what they *permit,* parents are usually very allowing of their only child. "This impulse to provide everything under the sun to one's child is especially keen in families where there's only one recipient of this passionate largess. Parents who choose to have one child know from the beginning that the first child will be their only one, so why not go all the way? . . . They can become gratification machines because they don't know any better."[4] The more a child is given to and given in to, the more she expects to receive what she wants and to get her way, the more willful she becomes.

A "controlling child problem" is usually a "compliant parent problem." Out of the desire to please, the fear of disapproval, the discomfort with conflict, or the inability to set limits, these parents:

- give in when they would rather refuse;
- go along with what they don't agree with;
- say yes when they wish they could say no;
- accept conduct they know is unacceptable;
- adjust to treatment they know is unhealthy;
- rescue the child from consequences of unwise decisions.

All of these choices are in the parents' control, not the child's. So who's got the problem?

Extremely indulgent parents can be guilty of extreme neglect when it comes to setting limits. They have a hard time saying no, and after having done so they often have a hard time sticking to it in the face of the only child's discontent at being refused. A "controlling" only child is often the outcome when parents mostly let him have his way, thereby grooming him to expect this indulgence in significant attachments later on. To prevent this eventuality, parents need to set three kinds of limits to help moderate their natural temptation to be unduly giving and permitting.

- *Social limits:* "We want you to have freedom to grow, but it will be less than you ideally would like, than some of your friends may be given, because of what we decide to allow. Sometimes you cannot do everything you would like."
- *Emotional limits:* "We want to hear how you feel, but expressed in a respectful manner. Sometimes you must exercise emotional restraint."
- *Material limits:* "We want to know what things you want, but you need to know you can't have everything you desire. Sometimes you will have to do without."

Setting limits is a major part of parental discipline, and it can be very hard to do with an only child whom parents do not want to disappoint or otherwise upset. In the words of one parent of an only child, "Disciplining or restricting an only child can feel like denying ourselves. What if we do something that makes her resent us? What if she thinks we are cruel or don't love her? Her misery is ours, and we feel it intensely, which is why it's so important to grasp what good discipline will mean in the long run."[5]

What "good discipline" does mean is training a child to discipline herself—to learn she does not have an unbridled right to get her way in relationships. "Discipline is a combination of parental instruction and parental correction that teach a child to live according to family values and within family rules."[6] Setting limits is how parents teach the discipline of self-denial; it is instruction that can be frustrating for an only child to bear.

As one adult only child explains, "This is how children grow into responsible adults, by being subjected to frustration as well as gratification. This is how children learn limits and understand that the world extends beyond them . . . Parents must be comfortable enough in their love so they can frustrate the child when it is appropriate."[7] *Parents can moderate willfulness through controlling gratification:*

- By delaying gratification they can create a *tolerance for frustration.*

- By denying gratification they can create an *acceptance of refusal.*
- By demanding gratification be earned they can create a *willingness to work.*

In the long term, the only child who receives excessive giving and giving into when young may carry that expectation into a significant adult relationship only to encounter a partner who will not continue the indulgent treatment it once pleased parents to provide. As one writer notes, "A child who is made to feel that she is someone exceptionally special will have troubles in making and sustaining relationships when two people need to be equal. This child would see a marriage of two people who are on the same footing as a demotion from the centre-stage and the spotlight."[8] So the best advice for an indulged adult only child entering a significant relationship may well be: "Let the demotion begin!" The notion of not being more entitled than the other person can be a hard concept to learn for an only child who grew up being put first by his parents. At worst, an adult only child who is determined to remain in control may select a partner who is submissive or dependent, creating a marriage in which dominance causes inequity and unhappiness as time goes by.

ADULTLIKE STANDING

It is true of any child that the more choice he is given in running his life, the more willful he becomes. The only child is given a lot of choice. "Households with only one child are often more *democratic* than homes where there are many children."[9] Without siblings, the only child is offered more choice. Democratically included in the parental world as a "little adult," she is given a more participatory voice.

One thirteen-year-old only-child subject put it this way: "When you are an only child, more time is spent with adults and you get a head start in growing up."[10]

An only child may not make parental choices, but she is often invited to have a vote in adult matters, such as family plans or even household purchases. What parents often don't realize is that every time they allow the child to weigh in, they are conferring adult standing on him, and by doing so enable more willfulness to grow. To prevent an only child from expecting dominant standing in later adult relationships, parents need to confirm her status as a minor in the family.

Treating the only child democratically increases the expectation of equality with adults. Sometimes parents let an only child have a say in what it's up to grown-ups to decide, and then they blame her for the willfulness they colluded in creating. Here's a prime example: Two parents came in with a complaint about their ten-year-old only child. "She's such a fussy eater! She never likes what we fix. Even if she liked it last time, she doesn't want it this time. We get so tired of offering her something else! The more we keep coming up with something different, the more dissatisfied she becomes. We just dread mealtime! How can we get her to eat what we prepare?" To someone reading this scenario, the answer is obvious enough: Don't give the girl a choice over what there is to eat. And don't get into a food fight over forcing her to eat. Instead, at supper calmly declare: "This is what there is to eat. You don't have to like it. But you do need to know that there will be nothing else to eat until breakfast. No snacking is allowed. It's up to you." Then they must mean what they say by sticking to it. In most cases a fussy eater is a child who has excessive choice about meals. Since serving a healthy meal is a grown-up's decision, the choice should not be given to the child. The situation's no different when parents complain that their only child teenager refuses to live on the allowance they provide and so they must keep giving him more. *Money buys choice.* The more money they give their teenager, the more choices he has to spend, the more willful he becomes about demanding more. *If parents want to moderate their only child's willfulness, they must limit the choices they allow, particularly those that are generally reserved for adults.*

Willfulness is also encouraged when parents exhibit the same willfulness they complain about in their only child. Highly directed and dedicated to raising their child carefully and right, they are often strong-willed themselves, a characteristic that serves them both well and badly. It serves them well because they are extremely intentional and conscientious parents, but it serves them badly because a lack of siblings causes the child to identify with highly controlling parents in the home. The equation "Like parent like child" is very influential with an only child: The way parents act represents the way the child wants to act. He loyally imitates their grown-up ways. So if, as parents, you have a strong-willed way, beware lest you beget what you will regret.

Identification with her parents causes the only child to want to "run things" the way adults do. Oftentimes, this willingness and willfulness to take charge is equated with a desire for leadership. Only children, used to directing their own lives, and yearning to run things like parents, are not shy about directing others. I have sometimes observed this in elementary schools when a small group of students have been assigned a common project for which all will share the same grade. If an only child is one of their number, she is likely to step forward and direct the collective effort, assigning responsibilities and usually doing most of the work to bring the final product up to her standards of performance. Research that compares only children with others has found that only children tend to show leadership in groups.[11] From what I have seen, I believe most of this "leadership" drive that some researchers and observers have often ascribed to only children is really *not* an expression of leadership so much as about "being in charge"—as their parents are and as the only child wants to be. *One of the unappreciated reasons why only children tend to achieve as highly as they often do is the willful engine that drives them to perform as capably as parents.* Another, as mentioned above, is identifying with their strong-willed parents.

STRONG-WILLED PARENTS

How can you tell if you're a strong-willed parent? In another book of mine I proposed that parents assess their own degree of willfulness by taking a simple inventory. Frustrated with their only child, it behooves them to determine whether the problem is *not* in the child but in themselves. The inventory I proposed was this.

How many of these statements apply to you?

- I don't take no for an answer.
- I don't back down to anyone.
- I hate losing an argument.
- I don't like changing my routine for other people.
- Once I make up my mind, I stick with it.
- Once I start something, I finish it.
- When I make a commitment, I keep it.
- When in disagreement, I tend to listen with my mind made up.
- I like to take the time to do things right.
- I get upset when I make mistakes.
- I don' like admitting mistakes.
- I don't like to apologize.
- I like other people to do things my way.
- I try to be perfect.
- I expect other people to live up to my standards.
- I don't give up.
- I will win at all costs.
- I need to know everything that is going on.
- I don't trust other people to take care of my business.
- I never admit defeat.
- I like to play by my rules, and I like others to as well.
- I'd rather give help than receive it.
- I don't like being told I'm wrong.[12]

If most of these statements seem to fit you as parents, then own the influence you are providing, as did one notable mother of an only child. In *A Life in Letters: Ann Landers' Letters to Her Only Child,* the author/daughter hears from a very strong-willed and wonderfully outspoken mom. "You being an only child have had all the heavy artillery centered on you. This has been both good and bad . . . especially when you have a mother who is a plenty strong personality . . . There is a lot more of me in you than you think . . . If you once make up your mind that you are going to do something, hell and high water can't stop you . . . I know I have a tendency to 'overdirect' . . . It's not easy to keep my trap shut."[13] Thus does a willful parent model willfulness for her only child.

However, if you want to moderate your willfulness as a parent to help your only child learn conciliation and accommodation, characteristics that are linked to *getting along with people* and not *getting one's way with people,* your behavior gives a powerful instruction. For example, while I was counseling two parents of an extremely oppositional only child, they wanted to know how to "make him" do what they said and not challenge and dispute them all the time. (Notice the term of control that they invoked.) They explained their situation: "We keep arguing with him to stop arguing with us, but his arguing has only gotten worse!" Of course, the only way to encourage a change is to change one's own behavior, starting with not arguing in order to get their way, just stating what they want or believe and not arguing back.

With an only child, how parents act is a lot of what they get back. Even if parents didn't act in a strong-willed manner, the child's identification with their adult standing and presumption of adult equality would still encourage his willful ways. The existence of multiple children in a family reduces the conforming influence of parents by creating a competing group of siblings to which a child can belong. Now the child no longer groups and compares himself with parents but with other kids (creating another set of problems through interpersonal rivalry). In the multiple-child family, parents can be "we" and the children "they." In the only-child family, there is no "they" the child can belong to; there is only the adult "we." "One of the functions of siblings is that with two or more children, the home becomes 'the kids' and 'the grown-ups.' The family encompasses two subgroups within the whole. With an only, there isn't such a ready-made division—parents and child are more blended."[14] In this setting, the only child may expect to be given the same freedoms as his adult companions. To counter this eventuality, it is recommended that "the family functions best as neither a dictatorship nor a democracy. Everyone can speak his piece, but the final word rests with the grown-ups."[15]

The only way parents can prevent this blurring of the boundaries between adult and only child is to *continually* clarify everybody's sphere of influence in the family. As an exercise, parents can do this by drawing for the child two vertical overlapping circles and then label each separate area according to who makes decisions there, giving specific examples of some choices made. Say something like this:

> In the top space, only your dad and I make decisions—like when we take time to go out by ourselves, how we spend money that we make, rules you are supposed to follow, and chores you are expected to do. These are grown-up decisions for us to make alone. In the middle overlapping space, you join us in the decision making—like helping decide what we do on family vacations, helping choose joint activities at home, selecting what you wear to school, and planning how to safely do a new experience. These are decisions we can all work on together. In the bottom space are decisions that belong to you—like whom you want for friends, choosing interests that matter, how you organize your room, and what you like to do to entertain yourself. These decisions you make independently.

By clarifying the differences between an adult and an only child in the family, the child is put and kept in her "non-adult" place, reducing the likelihood of willful entitlement that comes from her feeling she should be granted the status of adult. Parents muddy the water when they give an only child a double message: "We want you to act grown up and remember you are still a child."

From an early age, because of identification with parents and parental encouragement, only children want to act and be treated as adults. "Being grown up is a major preoccupation for only children as it is for first-born children, all their lives."[16] The only child, identifying with parents, but always having less than they, always wants more. To be treated "as a child" by them is usually offensive because it violates the mini adult role the child is striving to fill. The only child grows up faster socially than emotionally (see chapter 3), because primary companionship with parents has more influence than association with peers.

Aspiring to occupy the parental role can be a problem for the adult only child in a significant relationship when he assumes this position with his partner. In marriage counseling, she protests: "Stop acting like my parent! I'm your wife, not your child! We're equal.

You're not the one in charge!" But he always wanted to be the provider, the caretaker, the family decider, and can't resist the opportunity for doing so now. Supporting his wife's objection, I suggest to him that by acting as parent and treating his wife as child he cannot make a happy marriage because that partnership requires *two equal adults*. If he really wants to be a parent, then some day they may both decide to have a child.

If parental indulgence and the drive to assume adult status are two contributors to the only child's strong-willed character, cultivation and of adherence to a strong sense of individuality is a third.

STRONG INDIVIDUALITY

Despite strong identification with parents and pressure to conform to their ways, the only child is given enormous permission and support to become "her own person," to determine the person into which she wants to grow. She is accepted and affirmed for who she is, allowed to form her own interests, develop her capacities, set much of her activity agenda, and create her own identity. With no other siblings to be compared to or compete with, she can define herself on her own terms, creating a powerful sense of individuality. And by identifying with *both* parents, she claims enormous freedom of gender definition, a contributing factor to the strong individuality she establishes. In the words of one adult only child: "One of the most important things about being an only child is the chance to escape role definition ... I was basically allowed to be everything I wanted to be."[17] Unsaid is that for this to occur, parents must adjust to that individuality, an adjustment the only child may continue to expect from an adult partner later on.

Dual identification with both parents allows the only child to incorporate characteristics of each. Irrespective of sex role stereotyping, "male" and "female" characteristics become blended in the child, who can then seem androgynous to some degree. As one writer observed, "Onlies tend to be more flexible in gender roles because parents of an only child have less traditional sex-role attitudes themselves."[18]

Fortunately for the only child, parents can afford to be more accepting and flexible with him than when there are many kids to manage (in a large family it's easy to impose standard rules). And they can afford to support and invest in more facets of the child's development than when the child is one of many. From this acceptance, affirmation, and investment what emerges is a child dedicated to the development and preservation of her individuality.

There are many autobiographical and biographical descriptions of people who happen to be only children. One of my recent favorites is ostensibly about a pet pig: *The Good Pig: The Extraordinary Life of Christopher Hogwood.* The author, Sy Montgomery, an adult only child, describes her unique and passionate love of animals that came to dominate her life from early childhood; that passion was accepted by her parents, who, though sometimes offended, still supported their only-child daughter's highly individual, animal-loving nature. "Animals have always been my refuge, my avatars, my spirit twins. As soon as I learned to talk, I began to inform people I was actually a dog. Next, for an entire year, I insisted I was a horse. It was not that I disliked people; some were interesting and kind. But even the nice ones were no more compelling or important to me than other creatures. Then, as now, to me humans are but one species among billions of other equally vivid and thrilling lives. I was never drawn to other children simply because they were human. Humans seemed to me a rather bullying species, and I was on the side of the underdog."[19] The book offers powerful testimony to this birthright of *individualism* with which an only child can be endowed, and how that uncompromising individuality can be expressed with absolute integrity in adulthood.

Sometimes the strong commitment to individuality can cause an only child to pay a social price; insistence on personal terms can get in the way of group belonging. When this occurs, parents can at least help the child connect choice with consequence. "Of course the decision is up to you, but it seems to us that when you refuse to join the game unless you are given the position you want, then the other children may not want to have you on their team." Parents can also resist the temptation of catering to the only child's individuality by arranging exceptions out in the world. By creating exemptions from normal social demands, they risk encouraging her belief that individuality entitles her to special treatment.

On the positive side, as committed advocates, parents try to make the world work well for their only child because they want her well taken care of, which she usually is. On the problematic side, the child may come to believe that she should receive a free pass through normal challenges in life because she is somehow more deserving than anyone else. So, for example, parents explain to their senior in high school that they could "pull strings" to help him get into the college of his choice despite less than required grades, but that they will not because it would do him no favor, given that he did not actually earn admission.

What do permission for and support of individuality create? According to one writer, only children "often seem to be independent or unconventional thinkers . . . Many only children talk about the singularity of their experience . . . It may be that the less traditional upbringing of the only child makes him or her more comfortable with individuality . . . An only child must find his own path, after all, not follow in advance of or behind a sibling . . . Freed from the confinement of traditional roles and a large family, many only children are just 'free to be me.'"[20]

From what I have observed in counseling, the willful hallmarks of pronounced individuality in the only child, particularly when adult, are:

- *Clarity:* "I know what I believe."
- *Conviction:* "I stick to what I believe."
- *Constancy:* "I don't change what I believe to suit other people."
- *Commitment:* "I don't give up easily and admit defeat."

Anyone who marries an adult only child should expect a very strongly self-defined partner, a person wed to individual ways of behaving and believing, someone who is clear and decisive about wants, and has firm opinions about what is true and right and best. If there is a wishy-washy adult only child, I have yet to meet such a person.

SUMMARY

Four dynamics cause an only child to grow up strong-willed:

- Parental indulgence.
- Adultlike standing.
- Strong-willed parents.
- Strong individuality.

It is by moderating these tendencies that parents can temper willfulness in their only child. They can do so by

- setting limits,
- treating the child as a child,
- minimizing exceptions to normal social conformity.

Also helpful is tempering the willfulness they find in themselves, since what they model is what they teach. The only child strongly identifies with how they act. Since the degree of personal choice granted in general, and democratic participation in adult choice in particular, affects the child's willfulness, parents can regulate the latitude of choice that they allow. Through the unpopular setting of limits, parent create a system of healthy boundaries within which the only child can responsibly grow. Parents, by understanding the conditional shift that only children tend to make, turning a "want" into a "should" and then getting angry when denied, have to help the child understand that wanting something very much does not mean the child must have it and so *should* have it.

When the adult only child demands indulgence as his due, when he acts the parent and insists on special treatment in an adult partnership, these expressions of willfulness can undermine the relationship he wants. Most adult only children have to scale back the amount of willfulness they learned in childhood to successfully make an adult partnership or marriage work.

7

ATTACHMENT

A Matter of Intimacy

There is an enormous opportunity for closeness between parents and their only child. Undistracted by other children, the focus they give each other allows for deep psychological intimacy. They come to know each other unusually well compared with multiple children and parents. With two parents, the only child gets a front row seat for seeing how a marriage works. With a single parent, the only child learns partnership skills of a high order. On the problematic side, however, is that the extremely close attachment with parents can allow feelings to become contagious and emotional enmeshment to result. The feelings of one party are easily taken on by the other. The triangular relationship of only child with two parents can be susceptible to interpersonal manipulations as two divide against one, while the only child's partnership with a single parent can become so primary that the chance for forming same-age friendships is reduced.

To say that parents and their only child tend to be emotionally close seems obvious. How could it be otherwise? The closeness they feel with one another is rooted in spending much time together, caring a lot for one another, and coming to know one another very well. The extent of closeness can become a point of contention. Being sent off to bed alone when parents have each other for company can seem unfair to an only child who resists these separate sleeping arrangements.

Concerned for the only child's well-being, parents remain devoted to providing love, security, and comfort. Testifying to this empowering attachment, most only children would confidently declare: "I can always count on my parents being there for me." *From relying on this secure base of attachment with parents, the only child's independence begins to grow.*

In addition to security, the great strength of closeness from attachment between parents and only child is the quality of *intimacy* that can grow up between them. One parent describes how intimacy is enhanced with an only child. "More intimacy is possible with one child. Parents 'speak' to one child more, not just in words but in behavior. They communicate more to the child because the child is watching them, learning from them, aware of them, learning to pick up subtleties of human behavior. The child may notice something and say, 'Mommy, you're in a hurry this morning,' or 'Daddy, why didn't you like the news tonight?' and the parents are delighted that the child noticed. The process works in reverse, too, of course. You don't often find parents of an only child feeling alienated from that child. They've kept in touch."[1]

Another parent puts it this way: "There's an intimacy there I can't imagine could have developed if I had two and certainly not eight children... We do more things together. Our daughter has allowed us to be part of her growing up. There's more sharing and better parent/child communication than I remember in my home growing up."[2] It is important to appreciate that intimacy between parents and only child is not simply from the child's inclusion in the parental world, but from parental inclusion in the child's world as well. There usually develops a deeper two-way sharing of experience between parents and only child than exists between parents and multiple children in a larger family. This is particularly noticeable during the adolescent passage when parents and an only child often retain a closer connection than multiple children, who are more likely to separate socially into peer groups.

THE CONTAGION OF FEELING

The emotional connection between parents and only children runs very deep, like that described by psychologist Daniel Goleman in *Social Intelligence*. He explains: "The brain itself is social... One person's inner state affects and drives the other person. We're forming brain-to-brain bridges—a two-way traffic system—all the time. We actually catch each other's emotions like a cold. *The more important the relationship, the more potent such 'contagion' will be.*"[3]

Because the relationship between parents and only child is given extreme importance, each party is very sensitive and vulnerable to the other's feelings. Goleman goes on to say that "moods are so contagious that we can catch a whiff of emotion from something as fleeting as a glimpse of a smile or frown . . . When we attune ourselves to someone, we can't help but feel along with them, if only subtly. We resonate so similarly that their emotions enter us—even when we don't want them too."[4]

Without having to be told, parents and only children can sense when the other is happy or troubled. When either is feeling upset, the other usually wants to help that person feel better. Until the upset party (parent or child) can recover, the helping party feels some degree of emotional distress. So in the children's book, *Here I Am an Only Child,* the child wonders "if Mom looks sad, or Dad looks mad as if he's in a bad mood, I keep wondering if it's my fault, and how will I cheer them up?"[5] *I'm not okay when you're not okay* can be one operating principle of only-child family life.

As two researchers observe, "An Only Child often takes on the feelings of others in a symbiotic relationship. If someone feels bad, the Only Child feels bad . . . It's very important for Onlies to know that others feel good for them to feel good themselves. That's why Onlies will go out of their way to make sure everyone is happy. Then they can be happy too."[6] Constant watch is kept and continual care is taken because the emotional well-being of parents and child is so dependent on one another. This is one source of the only child's *emotional restraint* that often accompanies her emotional sensitivity and causes her to keep disclosure of unhappiness under control. "Don't you ever feel upset?" asks a partner who rarely sees his only-child partner act distressed. The answer is yes; the only child is extremely emotionally sensitive in attached relationships but has learned over the years not to always let her unhappiness show.

This skill was acquired to avoid an emotional bind with parents. When the child expressed unhappiness, the parents felt that pain on her behalf, leaving the child feeling guilty for the parental suffering that her expression of her own unhappiness had caused. Then she felt responsible for making them happy again. "But I'm feeling better now!" After they have gone through this sequence a few times, many only children learn to keep a certain amount of unhappiness to themselves.

Parents and only children can be very emotionally protective of one another. So the middle-school child doesn't tell her parents about the fight with her best friend today because they would just get upset on her behalf and she would rather spare their feelings. Occasionally I've seen an only child resist counseling out of the fear that seeking help might imply some deficiency in parental care or reveal a problem the parents might have caused. The child does not want them to feel implicated in her suffering.

Why would only children and parents be so attuned to one another's hurts? *The answer is that both lack sufficient independence to be able to care about each other's feelings without partly taking them on.* This is why, when a parent is prone to depression, anxiety, anger, or pronounced mood swings, it is good for them to seek some psychological help. Remember that part of what you primarily give your only child is your sense of well-being. Not only is help important for the afflicted adult, but also for the only child, who may need counseling to develop sufficient *emotional detachment* and *boundaries of responsibility* so that he is not overwhelmed by his father's or mother's emotional state. As two writers suggest, "Family troubles and parental shortcomings 'converge on the only child.'"[7] "Whatever the family is like, the only child within it receives the concentrated force of all its influences."[8] One parent worked out five statements to say (and mean) to her concerned only child to help the daughter stay emotionally detached when the parent was having another bout with depression.

- "When my hard times come, you need a way to take good care of you."
- "I have had these down times before, and I know how to help myself."
- "You didn't start my unhappiness and you can't stop it; that is up to me."

- "It doesn't help either of us for you to take my feelings on."
- "As I start feeling better again, I will let you know."

It really helps when parents have taught the child that emotional sensitivity to one another does not have to beget emotional responsibility for the other. It helps the child at the time and the adult only child later on. If a child can learn to allow a parent to be in a bad mood and simply let that person be, taking what time is needed to restore emotional well-being, then the adult only child is equipped to do so with a partner later on.

For parents and only child, the greatest risk of intimacy is that they become *too close for comfort*.

EMOTIONAL ENMESHMENT

What is too close for comfort? For the only child it arises when *emotional enmeshment* in the life of parents, separately or together, comes to preoccupy, dominate, or determine how he feels. It occurs when the child, in order to feel better himself, must find a way to fix unhappiness within or between the parents. It occurs when the child takes responsibility for parental well-being and faults himself when he is unable to make things right. It occurs when the child links his emotional state to the emotional state of the parents, who are often doing the same with her. *Emotional enmeshment begins where responsibility for emotional independence is given up.* Here are three examples of what I mean:

- "My dad could get so discouraged and self-critical, I had to cheer him up and give him lots of praise. My job was to get him feeling good about himself when he felt bad."
- "My mom was always so guilty and easily depressed when anything went wrong, I had to give her constant reassurance that she wasn't to blame, and keep encouraging her no matter what. My job was to keep her going when she wanted to give up."
- "My parents were incompatible in so many ways—different likes and dislikes, different temperaments, always grating on

each other. I was the only reason they stayed together, so it was my job to act happy to make them as happy as I could. I felt their marriage depended upon me."

Only children can be both beneficiaries and victims of intimacy with parents. Here are some warning signs that parents can look for to discover if intimacy is enmeshing the only child in their emotional life.

- Does the child act anxious—look worried, repeatedly ask what is wrong, or cling for security—when parents become upset with each other or with themselves?
- Does the child's mood seem to rise and fall with parental moods?
- Does the child try to cheer everybody up, divert attention, or attempt to figure out and fix the parental problem?
- Does the child act as mediator in parental conflicts?
- Does the child automatically apologize when either parent is upset?

If the answer to any of these questions is yes, then the parents have some important self-evaluation and explanation to do, attempting to reset limits in both cases. In *self-evaluation* they can ask themselves: "Are we depending on our only child to take care of us when we are suffering from emotional duress? To make us feel better? To take our mind off our problems? To distract us from tensions with each other?" If so, they need to take that responsibility back.

In *explanation,* they can declare something like this: "We appreciate how you want to take care of us when we feel unhappy with ourselves or with each other. But we want you to know that it is not your job any more than it is your fault. Like everybody else, we will have our ups and downs, and most of them have nothing to do with you. Our feelings are not yours to fix; they are for us to manage. When something feels wrong in ourselves or in the marriage, we will tell you so you don't feel you are imagining. But for privacy, we may not say exactly what it is. We will, however, tell you when we have worked it out and are feeling better."

This is a lot to expect a young child to understand. Only children, however, have a maturity of understanding upon which parents can often presume. The main point is to free the child up by establishing sufficient separation so that the boundaries of emotional independence and responsibility remain clear.

What further shapes attachment issues between parents and only child are the different dynamics that come into play depending on whether the family is headed by one parent or two. Start with the two-parent family first.

THE TWO-PARENT FAMILY

There is a sense of luxury with an only child. Parents don't have to worry about providing for one child at the expense of another, or having to fairly divide resources among contesting children. Parents can continue to indulge their preoccupation with the child who has brought them together in a new way. Before the child arrived, they were just married as partners, as wife and husband. Now they have become married as parents, as mother and father. *Because the only child has birthed them into parenthood, he or she is treated as integral to this new experience of intimacy between them, part of the parental union in this way.*

I think most of the adult only children I have counseled would own most of this description of what the relationship with their parents was like. "Particularly when I was a young child, there wasn't much social distinction made between my parents and me. They were linked to me and I was linked to them. I always felt attended to by one of them or the other. As I grew old enough to have opinions, I was consulted in family decisions. I rarely felt left out. If they were sitting on the couch, I snuggled in between. If they were talking, I was made part of the conversation. If they went off to do something, they usually took me along. I was really made to feel a part of them. I guess if you had asked me about their marriage, I probably would have said it included me in the middle."

There are significant strengths derived for the only child from marital inclusion.

- There is an enormous sense of *security* that comes from being so deeply anchored in the parental relationship.
- There is a sense of *intimacy* that allows the child to feel deeply known and to deeply know the parents.
- There is a sense of *standing* with parents that encourages the child to be outspoken and not be intimidated by their adult authority.
- There is an experience of *inclusion* in parental conversations, in parental social relationships, in parental activities outside the home that provide the child with enormous exposure to the adult world.

One adult only child describes a difficult side of growing up with two parents at home this way: "Three was an unlucky number, an awkward number, always two to one. We were a hopping, three-legged mutt, instead of a graceful, bounding retriever. There could be oppressive silences with only three people in an apartment. Honest hustle and bustle was hard to come by. Rambunctiousness, with its tripping, unabashed syllables, was not a word associated with our home. My father didn't roughhouse; my mother didn't tickle me until I screamed."[9]

The intimacy of the dual parent–only child triangle has been well described. "An only child usually has a strong voice in the family, so it's not surprising for her to think that she is an integral part of her parents' relationship. Two parents and an only child form a triangle—with the only child at the top. If she is allowed to take sides in quarrels between parents or thinks that she should be the one to settle things, she is taking on an adult role not appropriate for her age or position in the family. If she aligns herself with one parent against another, the structure becomes unbalanced...Only children are often sensitive to their parents' relationship in a way that kids with siblings are not."[10]

In this inescapable triangle, parents must strive to observe three priorities to preserve trust and provide comfort in a family system that can otherwise become unbalanced, unstable, and unsafe.

- Keep the unions strong. *There is no competition between parental and partner love.*

- Keep the separations clear. *There is no confusion between adult and child roles.*
- Keep free of manipulation. *There is no ganging up, no divide and conquer.*

The best way to keep the ill effects of triangulation from occurring is to continually mix people up by creating opportunities for every possible combination. Make time for all three together (family time). Make time for parents with each other (marriage time). Make time for each parent with the child (solo parenting time). Make time for each person alone (individual time).

In the dual-parent household, an only child identifies with the adults, strives for inclusion in their world, and sees herself as part of the parental "we," not the child "they" because there is no "they" to which the only child belongs. To her, the parental marriage is not limited to a relationship between two adults, but is a collective one that encompasses all three people, one in which the only child has a vital interest, holds significant standing, and plays a vital part. *A continuing challenge for parents is to include the child within the family while maintaining the child's separation from the marriage.* Separation reduces the temptation of the only child to presume and assume partner status in the parental union. Parental dating or socializing with each other helps make this distinction clear.

One psychologist recommends "Taking time for yourself as a couple—to go on an outing, to have a grown-ups–only conversation—is not being unfriendly and is not exclusionary to your child. On the contrary, it gives him critical opportunities to experience the adult/child distinction and to recognize that the two grown-ups he's so attached to have a special relationship that doesn't have to do with him . . . Just as Mom and Dad need twosome times, it's healthy for mother and child and father and child to step out of the triangle on occasion . . . It is good for your only child to enjoy times in the exclusive company of one or another parent."[11]

It's very complicated. By including her in their world, parents treat her as more adult than child. But to keep her from assuming partnership status in their marriage, they must distinguish caretaking responsibilities. "It's our job to parent you; it's not your job to parent us." Only children who have been given a lot of equal standing with parents in the family, particularly of the caretaking kind, can become adults who shoulder enormous, and sometimes excessive, responsibility in partnerships and in families of their own. The urge to "run things" that a partner may find offensive is often traceable, not to the only child's selfish drive to power, but to an obligation to take a lot of responsibility for those he loves.

One parent reflected: "The Threesome... is more open than relationships in multichild families. Parents talk to the only child in a more adult manner earlier and he is included in more adult events than children with siblings."[12] With the addition of a second child, *the sibling shift* takes place as the only child becomes one of two of "them" (the children), no longer one of "us" (the adults). Now parents make role distinctions between adults and children clearer, creating more social separation from the children, articulating more inequality, and limiting children's access to the adult world in ways it was not for the oldest child before. Another part of the sibling shift is the parental expectation that the child will be more self-sufficient, better able to do for himself than before. As two researchers further explain, "When a couple have a second child they are more than ready to encourage the first to act independently. The new baby needs the loving care that the old one has had, and there is just not time to give the same care to both. The older child is pushed out of the nest and must begin to exercise the ability to care for himself."[13]

As more independence is expected of the child, and his inclusion is lessened, the child's intimacy with parents is reduced. More children in the family mean there is less focused individual time with parents, and less knowing each other as well.

In a two-parent family, unity of the threesome is always kept in mind. Come divorce, that unity is broken. Now the only child must usually get used to living in two single-parent families at the same time.

DIVORCE

When parents divorce, they will have to deal with the child's grief at the loss, his anger at the betrayal of family love, and his fear of a future no longer secured by the parental unity he had come to trust. In addition, for the child's continued well being, they must reach an emotional acceptance of each other and commit to a social alliance that supports his ongoing care. Parents must emotionally reconcile as soon as they honestly can. They must come to terms of acceptance of the differences that drove them apart and the hurt feelings that were experienced so the child will not be caught up in any crosscurrents of ill feeling between them. Parents must also reattach to each other out of shared love for the child by forming a working alliance in support of the child's ongoing best interests so she knows that, though forever divorced as partners, they are committed to working together as parents on her behalf. How should they work together? By agreeing to abide by a code of conduct that allows the child to feel secure when she is moving back and forth in a two-household family. This code of conduct I called "The Ten Articles of Consideration" in my book about children and divorce, and it reads like this:

1. I will be *reliable.* I will keep the arrangements I make with you and the child. You can count on my word.
2. I will be *responsible.* I will honor my obligations to provide for the child. As agreed, I will provide my share of support.
3. I will be *appreciative.* I will let you know ways in which I see you doing good for the child. And I will thank you for being helpful to me.
4. I will be *respectful.* I will always talk positively about you to the child. If I have a disagreement or concern, I will talk directly to you.
5. I will be *flexible.* I will make an effort to modify childcare arrangements when you have conflicting commitments. I will try to be responsive to work with unexpected change.
6. I will be *tolerant.* I will accept the increasing lifestyle differences between us. I will accept how the child lives with us on somewhat different terms.
7. I will be *supportive.* I will back you up with the child when you have disciplinary needs. I will not allow him to play one of us against the other.
8. I will be *involved.* I will solve problems with you when the child gets into difficulty. I will work with you to help him.
9. I will be *responsive.* I will be available to help cope with the child's emergencies. I will be on call in times of crisis.

10. I will be *reasonable*. I will talk through our inevitable differences in a calm and constructive manner. I will keep communicating until we work out a resolution that is acceptable to us both.

By subscribing to the ten articles of consideration, you model behavior that you encourage in return, and you strengthen the alliance with your ex-spouse, as he or she is encouraged to do with you.[14] You don't have to like each other, but you do need to work together for the sake of your only child.

Come divorce, two single-parent families with an only child have been formed, and different parent-child attachment issues have been created.

SINGLE-PARENT FAMILY

A psychologist cautions that "A family of two provides unique companionship and with it the danger that your life and the child's life can become intertwined . . . It's especially difficult to define and separate the roles because of the intensity of the two-person relationship."[15] When, by partner abandonment, death, or divorce, a single parent assumes sole day-to-day responsibility for an only child, an increased bonding with each other is usually created. For support and security, the single parent and child become exclusively dependent on each other. In consequence, the child may think, or the single parent may actually say: "It's just the two of us, so we need to stick together." From this mutual reliance, a sense of *partnership* develops, and from it certain strengths can grow, but also a vulnerability when all you have is each other. As pointed out by one writer, "One of the disadvantages of being a lone parent with an only child is that you can become quite isolated and then you rely too much on each other for company . . . It's vitally important for both your own and your child's well-being that you maintain as many social contacts as you can, especially with grandparents and aunts and uncles and close friends."[16] Maintaining family ties contributes enormous emotional and social stability by letting the only child know that beyond the single parent a network of extended family and adult friendship connections is firmly in place. This way, the only child can confidently say: "We have each other, but we are not all we've got." Divorce is much scarier for the only child whose only "family" connection is his single parent. If it's just "us against the world," the single parent–only child attachment can become extremely close and self-protective.

In a two-parent household, a lot may be done for the only child. Satisfying her desires often becomes a primary focus of parental concern. In a single-parent family, however, indulgence of the only child tends to be qualified by a higher priority—the well-being and survival of the family unit. Usually the child is enlisted in a partnership to support the family by undertaking more household tasks and assuming greater responsibility for himself. Awareness of larger family needs is created by these contributions. A single parent often demands more work from the child after a divorce (compared to the only child in a two-parent family), grants less freedom of choice about household contributions, and will likely insist that the welfare of the unit comes before the pleasure of the child.

As one single parent explained it to me in no uncertain terms: "Look, I'm the only parent around here. If I put my child on a pedestal and cater to her needs at the expense of our own or my own, the family would collapse. I have to keep my priorities straight: It's me first, we second, and she third. When I'm too tired to do what she wants or what we need at the moment, she's got to let me rest. And when I need her to help out, she does." *For many only children, transition from a dual- to a single-parent household feels like a promotion and a demotion in family status at the same time. The promotion is being given more responsibility in the family. The demotion is learning to subordinate self-interest and accept less individual importance for the sake of the unit's good.*

The promotion to partner status with the single parent can both empower and intimidate the child. One only child described it well: "When my father moved out, things really changed at home. I was only eight years old at the time, but all of a sudden I had a different relationship with my mother. She would ask *me* things like what I thought we should have for supper or whether I thought a dress looked okay on her or whether I wanted to see a certain movie. In some ways it was fun. I felt important, like what I thought really mattered. But in other ways it was hard. Sometimes I didn't want to be the one to decide. I wasn't always sure of myself enough to feel I could make a decision."[17] The promotion into partner status confers on the only child more latitude and grown-up choice than an only child living with both parents, and of course much more than a child with siblings in a two-parent home. Hence the riddle: "When is a child *not* only a child?" In the single-parent home, the answer is: "When she is an only child."

As one only child described it: "Everything changed when we lost Dad. I had to grow up in a hurry. I became man of the house because Mom had to depend on me. It was hard, but not all bad. She treated me like my opinions mattered and my help made a difference. I learned to do a lot and felt good about myself." In single-parent households, only children tend to develop more responsibility at an earlier age than do their counterparts in two-parent families. Because more independence is required and more help is needed, an additional measure of competence and confidence is gained.

Another significant strength the only child frequently acquires in the single-parent home that goes along with responsibility is *reliability*. From acting as working partner with the single parent, the only child also learns to become a person who can be depended on, someone who keeps commitments. This reliability tends to stand the boy or girl in good stead in significant relationships, on the job, and in marriage later on. *Marry an only child of a single parent, and you usually wed someone well trained to take responsibility and keep her word.*

On the down side, a psychologist suggests, there can be risks. "Problems may arise, however, when either parent looks to the youngster to satisfy most of his or her own needs for warmth, affection, and companionship. Here's how that may happen—the three most common ways single parents of only children may tend to blur the line between adult and child: The only child as comforter . . . The only child as confidant . . . The only child as pal."[18]

The relationship between single parent and only child requires another caution. "In a family where there is only one parent, that parent might want to be the child's best friend. While there is nothing wrong with being friends with parents, it is important to have friends your own age."[19] The more "friend" an only child is to a single parent, the less easy it can become to make friends his own age. Growing used to the more mature companionship of a primary adult makes it harder to feel comfortable with peers who, by comparison, seem immature. The more *possessive* of that friendship the child grows, of course, the more difficult it becomes when a single parent wants to partner up again. So the injunction is this: The more your only child is your friend, the more effort you must make to immerse him in the world of his peers (where he is likely to attach to other only children, or to others who are more mature).

I have sometimes seen an only child's possessive history with a single parent cause her to be extremely possessive with an adult partner later on, reluctant to share that person with his biological family, with friends, with social opportunities out in the world. As one partner married to such an adult only child described it: "Only children take years to come to terms with sharing, and in some cases never come to grips at all. In a relationship they are much more possessive of the person—'*You're* my *other half*'—*and you feel you yourself have to be the beginning, middle, and end for the other person, you have to be sufficient for all that other person's needs.*"[20]

When it comes to preparation for marriage, single- and dual-parent homes each offer the adult only child a different advantage. Growing up in a dual-parent family, the only child sees a model for how marriage can be made to work. Of course, if the partnership is one in which parents routinely mistreat each other and accept that mistreatment, the adult only child is at risk of carrying those damaging and destructive behaviors into a marriage of her own. Short of that, however, seeing that parents get along and how they get along is positively instructive.

Because two parents may focus on the child more than the child on them, "it may be difficult to get the knack of moving in tandem with another person."[21] That ability is often better learned with a single parent with whom an only child may learn to partner or "move in tandem" very well, although the model of a working marriage is lacking, the attachment to the parent is intense, and the standing of the child more adult.

Finally, notice the prominence that you attach to your only child. Of course you love and prize her, but do not make her your "everything." Beware such statements as these:

- "You're the most important part of my world!"
- "Nothing matters to me more than you!"
- "You are my whole life!"

You may be at risk of great disappointment when you do not get comparable mattering in return. In the words of one only child, "Children always mean more to parents than parents mean to children . . . As much as I loved my father and mother, I don't think it approached their love for me."[22] The purpose of your parental love is to prepare her to love herself as a child and later as an adult and, if she so wishes, to commit to a partner who matters more to her than you.

SUMMARY

One benefit of the close attachment between parents and only child is a degree of *intimacy* less commonly experienced between multiple children and their parents. They are so well attuned to each other that *emotion can be contagious* between them, catching each other's moods, both ups and downs. Attach too closely, however, and emotional independence can be lost to *emotional enmeshment,* where one party cannot be unhappy without the other experiencing that feeling, too. For one to recover from suffering or hurt, the other must be made to feel better, too. An only child who has not been taught emotional independence is at risk of becoming an adult who becomes emotionally enmeshed in similar relationships later on.

In addition, what parents perhaps cannot teach, but what the only-child adult must learn, is the difference between the unconditional love received from parents and the conditional committed love that a partner will provide. For example, parents may have unconditionally loved their only child, tantrums and all, but a loving partner may conditionally refuse to accept that behavior in a healthy marriage.

In the dual-parent home, attachment can be complicated when triangulation occurs, two ganging up on one, one dividing two, or two ostracizing the third. To prevent family attachment from being endangered in these ways:

- the three pairs of two must be kept strong,
- the adult-child separation must be kept clear,
- and family unity must be well maintained.

In the single-parent home, attachment to the only child is even more powerfully made because without an adult partner for the single parent, the child is to some degree promoted into that role. From this promotion, the child usually develops traits of responsibility and reliability that often serve her well in later adult partnerships, but some degree of possessiveness may arise, and that may not serve at all. Finally, there may be more feelings of obligation in the adult only child to a single parent than to dual parents who can take care of each other.

8

CONFLICT

A Matter of Inexperience

M ost only children, willful and controlling though they may be, are not naturally combative. They don't enjoy conflict with parents. They shy away from conflict with peers. And they generally dislike conflict with their adult partners and will do much to avoid it. They are not the kind of people who go around provoking arguments to create a good fight. On the problematic side, however, because they lack the jousting and jostling with siblings that make getting into tussles and getting over them routine, only children are often inexperienced and uncomfortable with conflict—to their cost.

Conflict is a very serious issue for most only children because they grow up inexperienced and uncomfortable with it. They don't want it with parents, they have no siblings to contest differences with, and they tend to keep friendships only as long as they are conflict-free. Consequently, they are unskilled in constructively conducting conflict, often at the expense of childhood friendships, adolescent romances, and adult partnerships or marriages. They don't have good skills for constructively confronting and resolving differences and don't learn to use conflict to create more adequate understanding and unifying agreement.

This ill-preparedness does not have to be so if parents understand the issues at stake and the guidance they can provide their child along the way. First and foremost, they need to examine their own attitude and approach toward conflict. Obviously, if they see conflict as negative, avoid it wherever possible, or, when unavoidable, resort to extremes of coercion or surrender to get it over with as quickly as possible, that is what they are going to teach their child. Instead, I believe it is far better to normalize conflict by accepting it as one healthy part of all family relationships. How is it healthy?

NORMALIZING CONFLICT

In family relationships and friendships, conflict is the process through which people confront and resolve inevitable human differences in their wants, perceptions, and beliefs. The purpose of conflict is to open up discussion about a difference in order to increase mutual understanding and then, if needed, to negotiate a change, concession, or compromise that both parties agree will help them better get along. If constructively conducted, conflict increases both the *intimacy* and *unity* of the relationship because the process is both a *communicative* and *collaborative* one that allows differences to be talked out and worked out together. After a successful resolution, parties can feel more knowing of each other and better known, and more securely connected by the settlement they have agreed to.

Conflict is complicated because it involves listening to, discussing, and trying to reconcile two different ways of looking at what happened or at what needs to happen. Conflict can be uncomfortable because it can become emotional, creating frustration when understanding and agreement are hard to come by. Because anger from frustration is easily aroused, emotional self-restraint is required to keep both parties from doing or saying anything in the heat of disagreement that could harm the relationship in ways that they might regret later. Resolving conflict takes patience and practice, and for people in caring relationships, like parents and children, adult partners, or close friends, learning to conduct conflict constructively is the work of a lifetime.

For children, how to handle conflict is largely taught through experience. From differences with parents, from clashes with siblings, playmates, and friends, children learn that conflict, or fighting, as they usually call it, is a normal part of family and social life that one periodically gets into, feels bruised by, but gets over, and then moves on. *For the only child, however, conflict may not feel or be normal at all.*

Many only children talk about the difficulties they had in dealing with conflicts or fights... "I had to unlearn a lot of reactions I had as a child that were not appropriate for a child and certainly not appropriate for an adult... For instance, the idea that if you have a fight with someone, you can make up. That was a novel concept for me. As a child, if I had a fight with someone, I went home. If I never saw them again, that was fine. Whereas if you have a sibling, and you have a fight with them and you go to your room and close the door, you still have to sit down with them at dinner. Ultimately, you have to learn to make up."[1]

The mutually pleasing company of parents doesn't create much opportunity for conflict. Peacefully getting along is what parents and only child try to do. With no siblings, there are no rivals with whom to compete and battle. Without much preparation from, tolerance for, or comfort with conflict at home, quarrels with peers can end more friendships than they sustain. This is why parents need to encourage peer group membership in the only child's life—to learn the give-and-take, the push and shove, the hurt and recovery of ordinary conflict from peers when there are no siblings to teach it.

As one psychologist suggests, "A child can learn from all those aggressive and rivalrous sibling interactions. If all goes well, he will figure out how to stand his own ground, fight back when the occasion warrants it, back down at other times. Ideally, he will learn how to do this without putting himself down or making the other child feel bad. He will get some practice in the fine art of compromise. He will learn that it's no fun to stay mad and that it helps to be a good sport."[2]

As for adolescence, that period of growth developmentally ordained for young people to contest parental rules and restraints for freedom's sake, only children tend to resist this rebellion because offending parents and earning their disapproval is scary. As two researchers comment, "The desire to conform that only children feel is stronger than the desire to rebel for many of them at the usual teenage rebellion stage."[3] Since the only child and the willingness to engage in conflict are not a natural match, even during the teenage years, it can help for parents to set and follow some safe rules for conducting conflict with the only child, and to constructively model normal disagreement in their marriage.

AGREEING HOW TO CONDUCT CONFLICT

In counseling, it is often very helpful to ask parents and their young child if they follow rules for healthy conflict. Usually they will answer that they don't know what those are, but I will tell them that they do. Call it the Golden Rule or the Rule of Reciprocity, it seems to be pretty universal. For example, in one form or fashion it is present in most religions around the world. Essentially it says: "Treat others as you want them to treat you." So I will ask parents and their only child, "When in conflict how do you want the other party to behave with you?" And we start making a list that looks something like this:

> Listen to what I say.
> Stick to specifics.
> Stay on the subject.
> Be calm.
> Be reasonable.
> Don't interrupt me.
> Don't yell at me.
> Don't threaten me.
> Don't walk out on me.
> Don't call me names.
> Don't make fun of me.

Now apply the rules of reciprocity: "How I want you to treat me in conflict is how I agree to treat you."

And these are just for openers. It turns out that it's really easy for parents and child to come up with rules for healthy conflict that allow people to feel comfortable when they disagree. What is hard is for everybody (parents included) to stick to them. That takes commitment. Making and putting this list into practice is particularly important for parents to do with an only child. He is less experienced in conflict than children with siblings and so he needs instruction from and experience with parents. Of course, this list must apply equally to parents and child. Double standards such as "We can interrupt but you can't" communicates to the child another rule, that people in power are not bound by rules they set for others. An only child is already particularly sensitive to issues of unfairness because of other double standards that create his inequality with parents, inequalities to which he objects and tries to close by growing up very fast. When it comes to the conduct of conflict, behavior parents model with the child is most likely what they will get in return.

For the only child entering adolescence (around the ages of nine to thirteen) it can be helpful for parents to predict an increasing amount of disagreement ahead as she wants to become a more independent person. By doing so, they signify that this is normal, to be expected, and is not something that is wrong or to be feared. They can say something like this: "As you become a teenager, there will be more differences coming between us because adolescence is the process of you and us growing socially apart. You will want more room to grow, but sometimes we will want to hold on when you believe we should let you go, and then there will be disagreement between us. As you push for more freedom and independence, we will restrain that push within what we think are the limits of safety and responsibility. The job for you and us at these times of disagreement is to keep connected with communication as we grow apart."

I believe the fear of conflict with parents partly explains why the only child delays separating from parents by pushing against their authority and pulling away from their company during adolescence. The child wants to preserve the comfort and benefits of harmony and to put off the increased conflicts that are usually required for more independence as long as she can. From what I have observed, many only children don't really begin adolescence until middle school or even high school, whereas this process of transformation starts unfolding for most children in late elementary school. When adolescent separation and opposition begin late, the issues that the teenager selects can be powerfully divisive—an educational, occupational, social, romantic, or cultural decision that parents are hard-pressed to accept or actively oppose. The issues concern independence and are truly worth fighting for.

At such times, parents must let the only child know:

- no matter how hard you push against us, you cannot push our love away;
- no matter how socially separate our lives become, we will always remain connected as family;
- no matter how deep our disagreements, we will keep talking and working them out.

How parents conduct conflict with their only child particularly during adolescence is one major source of instruction for the only child. Observing how parents manage conflict in marriage with each other is another.

CONDUCTING MARITAL CONFLICT

How much parental discord should parents let the only child see? The answer is not simple. As one psychologist notes,

> Most children hate it when their parents fight. Only children hate it *and* they can feel terribly alone and abandoned, with no one with whom to share their feelings of fear . . . As grown-ups, however, we all know that occasional fights are part of life, because anger is part of life. And most children are relatively resilient individuals who, even though they don't like it when it's going on, will not suffer from normal levels of anger in their home. In fact, a youngster gets a critical, real-life learning opportunity when she sees, in her home, that people who love each other have differences and conflicts, and they can work them out and solve problems together. It is how parents handle fights that makes the difference in how successfully children deal with their own feelings about the whole thing.[4]

When parents protect their only child from any hint or display of marital disagreement, the child does not learn to accept conflict as normal and is deprived of an opportunity to see conflict successfully encountered and resolved. I'm not suggesting that parents stage fights for their only child for his instruction, but I am proposing that the child can benefit from witnessing healthy marital conflict. Suppose, for example, the only child sees this sequence of conflict unfold.

- Parents express disagreement with each other over something that happened or something they want to have happen.
- Parents get safely animated over the problem.
- Parents listen and exchange opposing points of view in a civil manner.
- Parents collaborate on an agreement that bridges the difference between them.
- Parents normalize their relationship and move on.

The adult child who says, "I never saw my parents have an argument or exchange an angry word," received no instruction in conflict at all. Later, in an adult partnership, such a child may believe that conflict should either not be started or must be stopped at once. In addition, when parents hide marital conflict from their only child, he will likely detect that something is going on and imagine the worst. In a world where divorce is frequent, it is common for children, only or not, to fear divorce when parents fight.

Parents cannot underestimate the power of their example for teaching their child how to safely manage emotional vulnerability in conflict. "Those couples who during their disagreements displayed more warmth, empathy, and mutual understanding also approached parenting together with greater harmony, even playfulness. And these parents had children who in turn got along better with playmates and could work disagreements out more productively. *How* couples work out their disagreements predicts their children's conduct, even years later."[5] For good and ill, this includes the adult only child.

There is a difference, of course, between an only child witnessing and learning from parental conflict, and an only child who becomes implicated or enlisted in the fight.

Knowing parents can have conflict and resolve it is helpful. Involving the only child in any way in that conflict is not. Just as the child is sensitive to his parents, he is highly attuned to emotional currents in their relationship. The downside of intimacy with parents is the only child's sensitivity to disharmony between them, and his tendency to take responsibility for trying to put the marriage right. When in conflict with each other, there are actions parents should *avoid* for the sake of their only child.

- Don't use the child as an emotional refuge or support when not getting along with each other. "Well, at least my child loves me."
- Don't blame the child for marital conflict. "We are arguing because of you."
- Don't ask the child to take sides. "Who do you think is right?"
- Don't complain about the other parent to the child. "He never does what he promises." "She never gets things right."
- Don't compare the child to the other parent in negative ways. "You're stubborn just like your mother." "You have a temper just like your father."
- Don't use the child as a weapon. "I don't know how you can call yourself a responsible parent and act this way in front of your child!"
- Don't use the child as a pawn. "Talk to your mother [or father] if you want to know why we've got money problems."
- Don't use the child as a mediator. "See if you can get your father [or mother] to forgive me."

Good advice for parents to keep in mind is this: "When you are tempted to make your child part of your marriage or involve him in marital conflicts, think again. Remember that your child loves you both equally and doesn't want to take sides."[6] *An only child cannot be pulled into alliance with one parent in the marriage without at the same time feeling disloyal to the other parent, extremely vulnerable to feeling torn and conflicted on that account.*

The most conflict-averse only children I have seen (both young and adult) are those who are the product of an unreconciled parental divorce. In this situation, where parental hostilities to each other are ongoing, the child often feels pressured to take sides, feels torn apart by opposing loyalties, and lives in constant fear of another parental fight. No wonder the child wants to avoid conflict at all costs in social relationships growing up, and in adult relationships with a partner. All the child has seen and felt is pain from the harm conflict can do.

Without adequate parental explanation, instruction, and example, an adult only child can enter attached relationships ill equipped to gain intimacy and unity through conflict with a partner.

THE ADULT ONLY CHILD AND CONFLICT

For adult only children in partnerships, conflict is definitely not easy.

- "Many only children referred to their inability to handle conflict and their difficulties in resolving disagreements. Many of them seemed to find conflict of any kind very difficult: *I'm bad at fighting and handling anger*... With your siblings you can 'practice' anger in a fairly safe way. But the single child has no one to practice with except his parents, and they are too risky because if he is angry with them they may stop loving him."[7]
- "The absence of squabbling and rowing with a sibling in the family... certainly puts only children at a disadvantage... they often simply do not know how to fight... lone children have no measure of what is the appropriate level of demand to make in a relationship—they haven't checked it out, they have no yardstick."[8]
- "As we have seen, many only children do lack skills to resolve conflict. Set this alongside their above-average ability as a mediator, and you often have a tendency to skate around the edge of family conflicts rather than be directly involved."[9]

Discomfort with conflict and not knowing how far to go, either avoiding any encounter or going too far by using extreme tactics to prevail, are the hallmarks of the only child's approach to this essential process through which significant relationships are continually readjusted, redefined, and renewed. From my observation in counseling as well, many only children seem particularly unprepared to constructively manage conflict in their adolescent friendships and adult partnerships. Some adult only children simply refuse to fight, either avoiding active conflicts using passive resistance to get what they want or get out of what they don't want.

Consider three common approaches to conflict I have seen adult only children take in partnership counseling. When a conflict occurs

- It's either flight or fight, but not *figure out.*
- It's conquer or concede, but not *collaborate.*
- It's my way, your way, or no way, but not *our way.*

Interviews with a variety of professional helpers conducted by only-child author Darrell Sifford for his chapter on "Marrying the Only Child"[10] suggest various causes for conflicts that adult only children can encounter in significant relationships, all connected with their experiences growing up.

- Conflict can arise from the only child's reluctance to share in relationship due to lack of practice.
- Conflict can arise from the only child's reticence to express personal thoughts and feelings.
- Conflict can arise from the only child's stubborn or unmodified individualism.
- Conflict can arise from the only child's self-centered need for special treatment.
- Conflict can arise from fear of abandonment.
- Conflict can arise from the only child's intolerance of being ignored.
- Conflict can arise from the only child feeling entitled to indulgence.
- Conflict can arise from the only child equating insufficient admiration with lack of love.
- Conflict can arise, when under stress, the only child demands more responsiveness from a partner when less may be available.

Given this list of an adult only child's possible predispositions to marital conflict, parents might want to modify the preparation they provide. For example, they could train the young child

- to practice sharing in relationships,
- to be comfortable with personal disclosure,
- to sometimes fit in and go along with what others want,
- to credit the needs of others as no less important than their own,

- to accept the impermanence of all relationships without fear of loss,
- to tolerate being in relationship when the focus is on the other person,
- to appreciate receiving special consideration but not feel entitled to it,
- to enjoy admiration but not confuse this expression of approval with actual love,
- to resist placing unreasonable demands on others when under stress.

In partnership counseling, where one party is an adult only child inexperienced in conducting conflict, there are a few guidelines I usually recommend.

- Do remember that to create and to resolve any conflict between you, you must cooperate: to both agree to disagree over a difference at the start and to both agree to support a settlement at the end, so working together is required from start to finish.
- Do treat conflict as an opportunity to use the difference at issue to better understand each other and to strengthen the collaboration between you.
- Do trust your partnership enough to appreciate that when it comes to understanding and resolving a conflict, two of you are smarter than one of you.
- Do listen to your partner well enough so you can state that person's point of view and position to their satisfaction.
- Do create a partnership in conflict where you are both on the same side (the ongoing welfare of the relationship) and not on opposing sides like enemies.
- Do use *specific* (not abstract) language in conflict to describe what you want or do not want to have happen, what you do or do not believe—ask the partner to be "on time," not to "act responsibly."
- Do treat your partner's opinion and self-interest as important as your own.

- Do discuss differences between you to better understand each other instead of creating competition by arguing to win.
- Do keep conflict *between* you and not *about* you—focusing on the matter at issue, and not on criticizing the "kind of person" your partner is.
- Do express concern for your partner's feelings in the matter so you can stay empathetically connected while disagreement is keeping you apart.
- Do commit to the principle that "listening to your way" and "finding our way" are more important then "getting my way."
- Do, after the conflict is settled, ask your partner what you did well during the disagreement and what you might do better or differently the next time you have a difference.

In many cases, the adult only child learns in partnership what she may have missed out on while growing up: to treat conflict as a normal part of life in an attached relationship, a process that can deepen intimacy and strengthen unity. From what I have seen, this preparation for the future of their only child is the one most frequently neglected by parents.

This is why in couple counseling I often give an adult only child a homework assignment—to write out all the meanings he can think of when considering this quote from psychologist Carl Jung: "Where love rules, there is no will to power . . . and where power predominates, there love is lacking." Why this assignment? To make sure that willfulness, which is another name for the "will to power," does not take precedence over "want to love" when differences arise. When it does, a power struggle can result, in which, by seeking control, the adult only child risks losing a valued relationship.

SUMMARY

The only child's lack of conflict with siblings, parents, and friends while she is growing up can cause inexperience and discomfort and avoidance of or overreaction to conflict in adult partnerships later on. This lack of preparation is not necessary. Parents can

- explain and instruct about conflict,
- model constructive conflict in the marriage,
- encourage participation in peer group play,
- anticipate more conflict with parents come adolescence.

Parents must not involve the only child in their marital conflict as pawn, weapon, or mediator. Finally, for the adult only child who received little preparation for conflict resolution with a partner, and who is at risk of going too far in his efforts to restore safety or to maintain or regain control, there are guidelines for what to do. Through practice, he or she can learn to deepen intimacy and strengthen unity when disagreements inevitably occur.

9

RECTITUDE

A Matter of Correctness

Rectitude (the sense of moral certainty) is highly developed in the only child. He has a strong moral compass that closely adheres to values his parents have lived by and taught him and with which he closely identifies. He tends to believe like them. Accompanying his sense of rectitude is a commitment to integrity—matching actions taken with values held. Not only does he have clear beliefs about right and wrong, good and bad, appropriate and inappropriate, he tends to follow them as well. On the problematic side, however, his commitment to rectitude can put him out of step with peers who do not share the same value orientation, particularly during adolescence. His tendency to believe he is right and to act righteous about it can alienate those who do not subscribe to his beliefs. And his ethical outlook on life can make him judgmental and critical. In close relationships, particularly as an adult, he can be prone to anger when others, in his view, do not behave as they "should."

When it comes to ethical opinions, only children are usually built from the ground up. By this I mean that from their earliest years they become staunch subscribers to rules and values communicated by dedicated and directive parents who are determined to instill in their child judgment about how one should and should not believe and behave. Part of having only one chance at child raising is wanting to do it "right," and part of doing that is teaching the child what the parents consider "right" beliefs and conduct to be.

Parents' moral standards contribute to the development of a moral compass in all children, but in the only child most powerfully of all—the boy or girl develops a sense of *rectitude,* of moral certainty, that stays with them through adolescence and into adult life. As one set of researchers reported, "The parents of one child may more easily be able to impose their ordered, adult values on that one child than can the parents of large families on all their children. This control, together with unchallenged values, may have contributed to the infrequency of teenage rebellion amongst our interviewees."[1]

The child who accepts deeply held parental values will not likely strongly rebel against them in adolescence. "In adolescence, they [only children] are less given to superficial conformity or disruptive rebellion. Teenage only children are more likely to retain the values of their parents than to become life-style rebels."[2]

More easily and lastingly imprinted by parental values, only children remain deeply committed to them as adults. These beliefs prescribe such codes of behavior as courtesy and manners, tastes and preferences, responsibilities and commitments. It's not so much the force with which these values are communicated by parents that instills them so deeply as that the child takes them on through unconsciously identifying with parents and consciously striving to emulate them. In the words of one writer about only children, "The joy of parenting one child . . . is raising a child who accepts you, identifies with your values. This may be the greatest reward parenthood has to offer."[3] Parents of an only child, and the child, usually do find this similarity rewarding. Parents feel fulfilled because what matters most to them is being carried on. Adopting these parental viewpoints and values is very tempting for the only child. Claim them and she comes to occupy the "high moral ground" of parents, from that self-assured position sometimes offending age mates with sureness that conveys superiority, acting like she knows best, which she feels she does.

Where children with siblings simply want to grow up, the only child wants to *act* grown-up, like the models he emulates, who in turn act pleased to see him assume their more mature ways. This mutual admiration society is self-affirming for all parties. It creates a sense of community that is more powerful than any that exists between the child, and often the parents, and anyone else. In consequence, the only child usually finds the parental world and worldview more culturally salient and influential than the world of peers to which, particularly in adolescence, most young people strive to belong as they separate into a community of friends. Taken into and brought up in an adult world as the companion of his mother and father, the only child often has more in common with the parents' culture than with the youth culture of friends. This identification can make letting go of family and fully fitting in with peers more awkward to do.

The price of not conforming to parents as peers may be disapproval or even exclusion, as it was for one young only child: "I still remember the time I criticized my parents for enjoying the card game I was growing tired of playing. After that, they didn't invite me to join them anymore, and I felt something was wrong with me." The only child soon discovers that although resemblance to parents is praised and rewarded, diverging from what they want can sometimes cause a temporary loss of good standing.

In families having multiple children, the increasing influence of siblings on one another gives the children alternative models to follow. As individual variation between children becomes apparent, parental tolerance for diversity within the family is increased, the pressure on a child to be like the parents is reduced, and full identification with parental values becomes less pronounced. For the only child, however, the individual values of the parents and the family values the parents share form the core of what he believes is good, right, appropriate, and correct.

When parents observe the child adopting their individual values, they can turn this to educational effect. They can explain how individual values can dictate personal behaviors that have a mixed outcome.

- Thus the mother may say: "Like me, you *value* having a lot of interests and love pursuing them all. A lot of interests keep life from ever getting boring. They make life rich. But I'd like you to know that I have paid a price for keeping up all the varied things I do. I've never committed the time and dedication needed to excel in any one of them."
- Thus the father may say: "Like me, you *value* speaking your mind. And that is good. In general, most people know where

you or I stand. They know what we think and feel. But sometimes, speaking up has gotten me in trouble, saying on impulse what on reflection would have been better left unsaid.
It's good to speak up, but it's also good to think before you
speak. Sometimes I've found it's even good to shut up, to keep
my reactions and opinions to myself."

Even when they encourage differences, parents tend to raise an
only child to be much like them. One adult only child reflected on
this during counseling: "I was never in any doubt about who I was,
what was right, what kind of person I wanted to be. Even today, my
values about right and wrong, many of my tastes, are pretty much
what my parents believe. They treated me so well and cared for me so
much, I wanted to stick to what they taught. That's why we're such
good friends now that I'm an adult. We had so much in common
when I was growing up, and as an adult we still do. I had lots of
teenage friends who fought to be different from their parents. Not
me." Echoes one only child subject describing his relationship with
parents: "We agree on a lot of things. Now that I think about it, we
rarely disagree."[4]

This high degree of agreement is not simply from the dislike of
conflict, as described in the previous chapter. It stems from the only
child's

- inclusion in the parents' world,
- identifying so closely with parents,
- conforming to parental wants and ways,
- incorporating their viewpoints and beliefs.

The only child's sense of moral certainty is deeply rooted in
parental values, and for the young only child and for the later adult it
provides a blessing of a very mixed kind. On the one side are characteristics such as being morally clear, principled, and determined to act
in accordance with one's beliefs. On the other side are characteristics
such as being rigid, dogmatic, and judgmental. The task for parents is
to help the child manage the strengths and vulnerabilities that rectitude creates, and for the adult only child it is to become aware of this

mix in significant attachments of his own. The complexity of managing this mix begins with the strengths and liabilities of having moral certainty and behaving with integrity.

MORAL CERTAINTY AND INTEGRITY

Opinionated is how most only children are. They are not vague or uncertain or ambivalent or confused about what is ethically correct. By adulthood, they possess a moral clarity and a code to live by, a *certainty* about what is proper, right, good, best, and wise. Because it feels important to live according to this code, the only child also has a lot of integrity, matching actions taken with values held. Why does she not betray the code? Partly because it would be a betrayal of parents and the values they represent. I believe that only children, in their similarity to firstborns, tend to be "more amenable . . . to their parents' wishes, values, and standards."[5] That is, they conform to and carry on the parents' cultural values to repay the high investment of attention and resources parents have made in them.

This determination to live with integrity can create a firewall against peer pressure during adolescence; the teenager refusing to be part of or to go along with what does not feel "right" with peers who are out for forbidden fun. So parents may applaud their freshman daughter's refusal to join a wild high school initiation put on by a cadre of older popular girls, yet feel saddened to see that in consequence of that decision she is left out of a major social scene. One reason why only children in adolescence prefer having a few like-minded friends to running with the crowd is that they find safety through socializing with people who share the same values and follow the same set of rules. Breaking the rules and being adventurous at this age can actually be hard for her to do.

"Rules" play a key part in how only children function. Following them is an act of loyalty to what they have been taught; they depend on these rules for security. They often act *legalistically* in the way they distinguish between should and should not, right and wrong, and are not shy about sharing the distinctions with others. For example, parents sometimes think that their young only child's insistence in making the rules for playing games when a friend comes over is a sign that their child is too fond of being in control, of dictating how others behave. From what I have observed, however, the issue often seems to be less about maintaining the upper hand than in doing things "right." Their child wants to make sure the "right way" is followed, to make sure that fairness, that hot button issue for most only children, is strictly kept.

My favorite response to the question, "How do you know you're right?" came from an eight-year-old only child in counseling who immediately replied: "Because I just am." That settled that! His absolute confidence was based on a certainty that rectitude had taught.

There is a sense of loyalty to his ethical convictions, as if the child were saying: "I know this because my parents taught me so." It is very easy for an only child to become a true believer in what parents state and represent. One adult only child explained it this way: "The only child . . . is so eternally influenced by what parents say and do. Children with siblings have daily reality checks . . . but the only child generally has nothing with which to counterbalance parental messages on a regular basis. If Mommy and Daddy say it, it must be so, the whole truth . . . Children are quite malleable, and they become like us in many ways. They adopt our beliefs, some of our viewpoints. Kids identify with parents."[6] And with only children, this identification is often strongest of all; similarity to parents is cherished by both parents and child because, by creating agreement and commonality, it keeps them close.

Identification with the parents also encourages the firmness with which these beliefs are held and the extremely clear distinctions these ethical judgments create. Values are absolute, not relative. They are fixed, not flexible. They are closed to examination, not open to discussion. And value distinctions are of the either/or kind. Ethical discriminations are black or white, good or bad, correct or incorrect. This strict framework makes deliberate wrongdoing hard to do—to step out of line, get into trouble, and do what has been forbidden. This is one reason why much rebellious risk taking during adolescence is less likely to occur with an only child. There is less fear of what parents would think of him and say to him and do to him than of how personal guilt would punish him for knowing he did wrong.

RISK TAKING

Outside of areas of special competence and passionate interest, where he can be very adventurous, the only child tends to be a low risk taker when it comes to challenging established rules or straying from what is traditionally valued. Obedient to parental authority because she identifies so closely with it, and having so deeply internalized its demands and restraints, she tends to comply with other authorities, at school for example, and become known more for following rules than breaking them, more for working within the system than challenging it. This is why she often gets a reputation for acting like the teacher's pet. She knows how to communicate well with this adult, to cooperate with her requests, to comply with her rules, and to conform to how she likes things done. The young only child may not be that comfortable interacting with peers on the school playground at first, but he is precociously skilled at getting along with resident adults.

Because they are bound by rules, only children are not generally very daring during adolescence, being cautious when it comes to risk taking, not getting into extreme experimentation, not violating serious rules, not adopting some dramatic alternative identity. For example, in counseling I haven't seen a lot of Gangstas, Goths, Punks, or Stoners among only children. Few are lawbreakers, or have bodies that are pierced or tattooed or hair that is dyed. As teenagers, only children tend to be relatively conservative, rule bound, and risk averse, although (to their parents' alarm) they may get into experimentation by association. That is, they may choose acquaintanceships with more alternatively defined or wilder kids in order to experience vicariously what they would never actually do. But for close friends, only children tend to select companions who are not the daring or dangerous kind. In fact, only children will take themselves out of social play if it feels too risky or wrong.

Sometimes acting with integrity exacts a cost. In fact, it may not even be wise. Consider this situation, and what you would advise as a parent. You have an only child in eighth grade at a middle school who has discovered that another student is bringing drugs to school to sell. Now your child is planning to report this fact to the assistant principal. On the one hand, you admire your child's integrity for doing the "right" thing and turning the dealing student in. On the other hand, you wonder if this action is wise since "narcing" on a peer might lead to physical reprisals from that student or some of his friends. What do you do? Well, at the very least you have a discussion with your only child about being a whistleblower and the dangers that it can entail. Doing right can be risky, and you don't want your child to fall innocent victim through his act of "good" intent.

The only child's sense of rectitude usually creates later problems in the form of value conflicts in adolescent romances and significant adult attachments. "Whose way is the right way?" can be a divisive question when, for example, his exclusive ("responsible") approach to having sexual partners conflicts with her free-spirited ("open") desires, and he lets her know the error of her ways by demanding that she only be intimate with him. As one psychologist who has spent a lot of time studying birth order observed, "Onlies tend to be critical... They become very impatient with, or very intolerant of, people who don't measure up to their standards. Only children often quietly (sometimes not so quietly) wish they could move in, take over, and 'do it right.'"[7] It is a hard distinction for parents to help their only child learn to make—the one that separates a conviction of rectitude from an attitude of intolerance that justifies acting in an overbearing way. To help the child avoid social hardships that can follow from his moral certainty, parents do not have to teach him moral relativity. Rather, they need to help him learn to expect and respect value differences. To do this with their preadolescent child they could explain something like this: "Because you and we are so close, we pretty much agree about how to act and what is right and valuable and true. With friends there will be more differences in outlooks between you and them than between you and us, and that is okay. To get along with other people you don't have to get them to change their beliefs or give up your own. You just have to make room for these differences between you by accepting them. Then focus on what you both can enjoy doing together."

As parents, support your only child's determination to stick to the values he has learned from you, but also encourage him to be tolerant of, and able to work with, the inevitable value differences with others. Particularly, help him pay attention to his use of two telltale words, "ought" and "should." When present in his thoughts and speech, they indicate that his sense of moral righteousness is up and running.

PEOPLE OF THE "SHOULD"

I tend to think of only children as "People of the 'Should.'" Their sense of rectitude creates a conditional view of how they and others are *supposed* to act. For example, from counseling, my impression is that there are core values that most young and adult only children would embrace that might include the baker's dozen listed below.

As an only child, I should:

- try hard,
- do well,
- do right,
- be careful,
- be above reproach,
- control what happens,
- be responsible,
- demand fair treatment,
- earn approval,
- follow rules,
- speak up for myself,
- act grown up, and
- avoid getting in trouble.

Only children tend to let conscience be their guide in directing themselves and in criticizing others. Thus the word "should" is an ever-present component of their thinking, and often of their speech. A consequence of this conditional thinking can be acting controlling to get conditions met and becoming angry when they are not. When a "should" is denied or violated, then a "wrong" has occurred, and a sense of "being wronged" has been created. So parents may want to help the young only child be aware how using "should" creates expectations that set her up for conflict or for disappointment with others. Here are some common examples of this conditional thinking.

- "If I believe I am right, others should agree with me."
- "If I have something to say, people should listen to me."
- "If I don't like how others are treating me, they should be made to stop."
- "If I want things done a certain way, others should go along with my wishes."

"My best friend didn't sit with me at lunch today like he *should* have!" complains an aggrieved seven-year-old only child to her parent after school. "I never want him for my friend again!" For this only child, friendship comes with a whole set of implied conditions which, when unmet, can arouse an angry response. Parents can help an only child, not by criticizing this tendency to look at life through a lens of what should or should not happen, but by accepting it, going on to explain the consequences of, and possible alternatives to, holding this conditional view. So the parent in this situation might say: "Just so you know, when you think your friend *should always* behave in a certain way, you're going to feel angry when he does not. But when you change 'he should' to 'I would like,' and 'always' to 'sometimes,' then you won't feel so hurt when he doesn't act the way you want."

Rectitude can create a "double should" in value conflicts with the adult only child. There is the "should have" from the *conditional shift* (when "what I want" becomes "what I *should* get") that is one source of her willfulness (see chapter 6), and then there is the "should be" that comes from conditions imposed by sense of rectitude. The result, as many partners of adult only children can attest, is running up against a *double should* statement in a value conflict: "You *should do* it my way because I know how it *should be* done!" Arguing against this statement, the partner may encounter anger on both counts, asking: "Why do you get so angry just because I *won't do what you want* and *believe you are wrong?*" Of course the answers are in the question.

There are really two "rights" that are often linked together by the only child when young, and by the adult later on:

- Conviction about knowing the *right way* is a matter of rectitude. "We should do it my way because that is correct."

- Conviction about the *right to* get one's way is a matter of entitlement. "We should do it my way because this is so important to me."

Parents have to teach their only child that *rectitude is not entitlement.* Give the young only child some help in managing the strong set of values with which he has been endowed. Here are some guidelines you might want to provide.

- Be clear about your values—about what is good and bad, wise and unwise, appropriate and inappropriate.
- Stick to your values. Stand by your principles and follow your beliefs.
- Use your values as a moral compass, but do not expect them to rule the world.
- Treat opposing values with respect. Believing differently from you doesn't make the other person "wrong."
- Don't make conforming to your values a condition of friendship now or of partnership later.
- Keep yourself open-minded enough to learn from the values of others.

Only children are constrained by the conservative values they keep. Their sense of rectitude has some protective value when it causes them to stay away from adventures on the wild side that may attract their more impetuous peers. They can stand apart from peers in a judgmental fashion, critical of how others behave, often relying heavily on evaluative language to condemn how others act. Seeing the world so judgmentally can also predispose them to more anger than people who are less ethically committed and conditionally disposed.

THE PROBLEM WITH ANGER

Only children can be anger-prone from

- being highly *controlling* (see chapter 6),

- being highly *sensitive* to real and imagined insults (see chapter 3),
- and being highly *judgmental* (this chapter).

Not getting his way, being easily hurt, and seeing oneself or others as not doing things right can all trigger anger in the only child.

It is the last of the three anger factors that is of concern here—the tendency of the only child to be highly judgmental, easily angered when what "should" happen doesn't happen, or what "shouldn't" happen, does. In either case he experiences a violation of the rectitude he holds so dear. In general, the more one's worldview is prescribed by conditional expectations like "should" and "should not," the more violations come one's way, the more one ends up feeling offended and angry because something isn't right, fair, deserved, or didn't meet the standard that rectitude had set.

So the only child righteously protests. "It's not *right* you won't let me go. I *should* be allowed to do what my friend can. That's only *fair!*" His right to equitable treatment has been violated and he feels betrayed and angry. Now parents have some explaining to do. "Just because you *want* something a lot doesn't mean you *should* get it. Much of what people believe is right in life doesn't work out that way. This doesn't mean you shouldn't stick to your beliefs. But pay attention to your feelings when life doesn't measure up. If you decide to get offended every time life doesn't turn out the way you believe it should, you will end up spending a lot of time feeling angry and unhappy, blaming others for not living up to the conditions that you set. Do you want that?"

This goes for the adolescent and the young adult as well. For example, in counseling, an outraged twenty-four-year-old only child explodes at her parents. "How can you stop my allowance!" when they propose to give her less money so she will assume more financial responsibility. "I'm still your child! I still *deserve* your support. You've been paying for my car and apartment all along, so you *should* continue. It's not *fair* for you to stop now!" She feels angry having her due denied. And the rest of that counseling hour is spent painfully hammering out a diminishing schedule of financial assistance. Whatever happened to gratitude for all they have given, the parents wonder. She is at the age when she is supposed to be acting more grown-up, and their daughter is still caught up in making a double-should demand based on entitlement and rectitude. The parents are helping her turn a right to support from them into a responsibility to take care of herself—thanklessly. When it comes to causing herself unhappiness, a sense of rectitude can be the only child's Achilles' heel.

As adults, assuming they learn in a partnership what they did not learn with their parents, only children may become less conditional in their expectations. They may become easier to live with as others find them less judgmental, intolerant, critical, controlling, and easily angered. And they may find themselves easier to live with in an important way—by becoming more accepting of their own errors. This brings to mind the observation: "Firstborns find it particularly hard to admit their mistakes."[8]

Like those firstborns, the only child may trust too much in the rectitude of what respected authorities such as parents have taught him and hold himself to extremely high account. His sense of rectitude can make the concept of "wrong" difficult to tolerate in himself and others, in a number of ways. It can be very hard

- to be wrong,
- to admit being wrong,
- to apologize for acting wrong,
- to make amends for doing wrong,
- to be wronged,
- to forgive being wronged,
- to see others do wrong,
- to withhold criticism when others do wrong.

Rectitude is a good servant when it provides a moral compass; but it is a bad ruler when no error goes unpunished. This heightened moral certainty is what can make the only child so critical of himself when misjudgments occur. It really helps to minimize the harsh side of rectitude if parents can model the normalcy of mistakes by admitting their own and accepting the child's without censure. From parents who are honest and easy with themselves and the child when errors are inevitably made, the only child can learn to enjoy the benefits of rectitude without suffering unduly from the costs.

SUMMARY

The only child's sense of rectitude, of moral certainty, is deeply rooted in his identification with, and incorporation of, parental values he often feels duty bound to carry on. Conforming in order to belong to these older family peers who treat him like an adult and approve his emulation of their ways, he has much more in common with them then with peers in his age group, even during adolescence.

Rectitude's mix of strength and liability make its management complex. The moral certainty creates clarity on one side, but risks rigidity on the other. The way the only child sticks to his principles creates integrity, but he risks becoming value-bound—doing what is right when it might not be wise.

In significant attachments, adult only children must learn to resolve value conflicts. They can do this by translating the value they have into the behavior they want, negotiating and compromising wants while keeping values intact. "Based on my values, this is what I want to happen. Based on your values, this is what you want to happen. Rather than arguing to change each other's values and defend our own, let's put the value differences aside and work out a compromise of outcomes that we can both live with."

Conditional thinking often frames decisions in terms of what *should* or *should not* occur, thereby causing the only child, young or adult, to become controlling in order to get conditions met, or to become anger-prone when they are not. It can be hard for the only child to learn that rectitude is not entitlement. To become less anger-prone, the only child can practice becoming less conditional in his outlook, particularly in his judgment and expectations of others.

10

AMBITION

A Matter of Achievement

Most only children are ambitious to achieve. They want to shine in their parents' eyes, and one sure way of earning parental pride is by performing well. In addition, they also find achievement affirming. They enjoy doing well for themselves. With the only child and her parents both expecting her to excel, the self-fulfilling potency of these dual streams of motivation is usually hard to deny. On the problematic side, however, is the child's feeling of relative failure when *unrealistic* ambitions are set and unmet, the child falling short of her own or parental dreams, feeling like a disappointment on one or both counts. At worst, she may be lured away from the healthy drive for excellence and into the unattainable pursuit of perfection, perfectionism being a troubling issue for many only children.

Although *ambition* is just one kind of expectation (and will be discussed as one of several only child stress factors in chapter 15), it deserves a chapter of its own because it is such a *huge* issue in only child families.

Not every only child is a high achiever, but most only children are ambitious to achieve. How could it be otherwise? With such a high parental investment of attention, time, and resources in their special one, there can come a high expectation of return—for the child to do as well by them as they do by her. There's a quality of self-fulfilling prophecy when it comes to this ambition to achieve: Parents are ambitious for their exceptional only child who, convinced of her own superior capacity and wanting to meet parental expectations, usually becomes ambitious for herself.

Even if a parent doesn't necessarily begin by thinking the only child is exceptional, the parent can be ambitious to make this so. The portrait of advice columnist Ann Landers drawn by her only-child daughter Margo Howard testifies to this determination. "I had no siblings and my mother was heavily invested in me...she felt that my persona reflected on her."[1] "It's fair to say that my mother was ambitious for me, in the sense that she was, in spirit, a stage mother...without the stage. She wanted me to do well and to shine."[2] In one letter to her daughter, Landers was marvelously forthright. "I am still your mother and it is MY responsibility to see that nothing spoils my masterpiece."[3] Along with a mother's absolute love came her unwavering ambition, not just for her child, but for herself as well.

As one adult only child commented, "For some parents, the greatest achievement of their lives is their child."[4] A mother of an only child put it this way: "Many parents have vicarious dreams for their children, but parents of only children have epic visions."[5]

Parental ambition is one explanation of why only children tend to be ambitious to achieve. There are others.

- "Many psychologists believe that it is, at least in part, *because* parents of onlies are so responsive to and focused on their children that those youngsters tend to become high achievers."[6]
- "Increased interaction with adults is one of the notable benefits of being an only child... 'that's why only children do better intellectually.'"[7]
- "Generally, only children have more educational advantages, no sibling rivalry, and more of their parents' time."[8]
- "Why do people have just one child? You might have parents who are very achievement-orientated themselves and they're not particularly interested in having lots of kids because they're busy doing X, Y, and Z. If so, then what they teach their only child is that what's important in life is to achieve. So there's the issue of value-transmission."[9]

What also fuels the only child's ambition is the adult family company she keeps.

THE POWER OF ADULT ASSOCIATION

Speaking up, expressing opinions, and being consulted about family decisions all feel like a birthright for the only child. Unintimidated by parental authority, the only child is often not intimidated by external authority either. Parental friends, with whom the child learns to socialize, usually consider him or her socially precocious and are impressed by adultlike manners and skills in one so young. "How grown-up you are!" is a common compliment they give. And the only child becomes adept at socializing with other adults on their level.

Rewarded for seeming older than his or her years, the only child usually learns to act more and more socially mature. In the words of one adult only child looking back: "Of course I knew I was a child, but I also knew that I was supposed to act grown-up. My parents didn't want to baby me because they didn't want to keep me acting like a baby. They wanted me to join their world as soon as I could. They treated me as a little adult, and so did I. They didn't pull rank on me, they explained what they wanted from me and why. Even though they made the rules, I was their equal as a person."

In consequence of being "adultized" in this way, the only child, usually unbeknownst to parents, then makes an intuitive and very formative resolve: "Since I consider myself to be their social equal, I should be their equal in other ways." *Still a child, he assumes equal standing with parents, applies equal performance standards, and becomes ambitious for equal competence as well.* Without the urging of parents, and with confidence gained from verbal and social precocity, this seems like a realistic thing to do. Because of this aspiring to adultlike competence, parents of only child usually need not, and probably should not, push or pressure their son or daughter to achieve academically. There is sufficient built-in motivation to suffice since the only child wants to close the gap between child and adults almost every way he can, as soon as he can.

Since the only child is usually so highly motivated, the parental job is to humanize this ambition. In doing so parents can speak to a number of issues that encourage a healthy perspective.

- When the only child gets upset at not being able to do a task as easily or as well as parents, they may want to gently remind her that she is not yet an adult. They have had more years to practice what the child is now learning to do for the first time. *"Don't measure yourself against us. That's not being fair to you."*
- When the only child shows signs of treating performance as his major measure of self-worth, parents may want to remind him that he is a human being first and a human doer second. *"Our love for you, and we hope your love for yourself, is based not on what you achieve, but on who you are."*
- When the only child is crestfallen after failing to meet a personal ambition, parents may want to remind the child that in the long run effort is more important than outcome, and that there is no failure except a failure to try. *"You always learn something from trying, and every effort you make only strengthens your capacity to work hard for whatever else you want to achieve."*

Parents have to draw a fine line between stressing the importance of achievement and overstressing it.

WHEN PARENTS ARE TOO AMBITIOUS

Parents must definitely guard against what can happen when their child's success matters to them too much.

Overambitious parents drive many an Only to desperation. The child is the parents' one connection with the future. They say that they want him to have everything that they did not have. Maybe they have refrained from having more children so they can give the Only every advantage. They hope to see the Only fulfill all their unfulfilled ambitions. They look forward to basking in the glow of his fame. Any failure in school, especially any shortcoming in academic achievement, seems to them a betrayal. They impress the child with the idea that if he is not first in his class he is letting them down.[10]

It is good for parents to remember to be sensitive to how much of their own aspirations are tied to the child's achievement. It is easy for them to let the only child's academic and other achievements become a measure of all the conscientious parenting they give: "How well our child performs shows how successful our parenting is." Most parents are ambitious for their only child. "We only want the best *for* you" can be a coded message for "We really want the best *from* you." I once heard an adult only child put it this way: "I was born expected to fulfill a promise to my parents I never made, but was supposed to keep."

At worst, parental ambition to raise a "trophy child" who will make them proud can place unbearable performance pressure on an only child, who may finally explode at his parents in anguish, saying something like,

> Stop doing this to me! You're loving me to death! The only way for me to be your perfect child is to lie. To pretend to be how I'm really not. My life is my life, it doesn't belong to you! I love you, but I hate having to work to make you proud. Proud of what great parents you are! I hate the responsibility. How you feel about yourselves all depends on me! I'm all you care about! I'm your whole life! Why don't you get a life of your own? Why don't you let me have mine? I hate having to be perfect to make you okay! I hate being afraid of disappointing you! Why do I have to be afraid of letting you both down? Why does it matter to me so much what you think? Why do I have to care?[11]

Parents of an only child must beware the pitfall of their own ambition—treating their child as a mirror of themselves. When parents have "dreams of glory" for their only child, the child, strive as she might, is usually left with the feeling that she's failed to make her parents look "good enough." They gave her all the support they could, and it is incumbent on her to give them back all the accomplishment she can. This sense of failure is acutely felt in early adolescence when the traditional focus on schoolwork often gets replaced by social priorities that are now felt more urgently by the child who is becoming more concerned with making good friends than good grades.

The five most destructive statements I have heard frustrated parents make to their failing or floundering only child, usually in middle school, are:

- "You're not even trying!" And now the child feels *shame.*
- "You really let us down!" And now the child feels *disappointment.*
- "You'll never succeed this way!" And now the child feels *hopelessness.*
- "We just give up on you!" And now the child feels *rejected* or *abandoned.*
- "All we've done for you, and now you do this!" And now the child feels *guilty.*

In all five cases, these statements were made by parents in response to an only child who had begun to "fall away" from traditional achievement by letting schoolwork slide during adolescence. The parents wonder: Has the child lost all ambition? What's going on?

The answer, often, is that the parents, spoiled by having a young only child who not only meets but often exceeds their hopes, can become upset when, in adolescence, the young person becomes less invested in or more opposed to serving the ambitions that the parents have held dear. A falling away in school achievement often accompanies early adolescent change. Now the young person, in late elementary or early middle school, actively and passively rebels against childhood and acts deliberately different in order to assert more independence and claim a new individuality. For most children, with siblings or without, *adolescence is the enemy of achievement.* Ambitions that parents and child shared in elementary school seem less important to the middle schooler. Now parents must encourage continued industry when the adolescent feels less inclined to work.

The statements of censure quoted above are not helpful in this regard. Parental criticism, to which the only child is particularly sensitive, only makes a hard situation worse by fueling resistance with resentment. It's not that the only child doesn't still want to do well; he just doesn't want to do the work. He hasn't lost his ambition, just the will to carry it out. At this point, it is better for parents to be nonemotional and nonevaluative if they want the young person to achieve creditable grades at school by maintaining adequate effort—finishing projects, cooperating in class, studying for tests, completing and turning in homework. More effective than complaints and criticism about the child's character is for parents to calmly focus on specific decisions the child has made and needs to make differently. "We disagree with the choices about schoolwork you have made. This is why, and this is what needs to happen in consequence." Failing grades result from failing effort, so the parents' job is to apply their supervision and support to increasing the child's application at school—completing all assignments in a thorough and timely way. "We will spend whatever time it takes with you, at home and even at school, to make sure that all your schoolwork is being done. We want to help you do as well as you are capable of doing for yourself."

Parents of an only child must remember that their ambition for their teenager to do well pales beside the child's ambition in this regard. Falling away is no fun for the child. She wants to shine in their eyes so she can shine in her own. Most only children wish they were perfect.

PERFECTIONISM

Years ago, a colleague described perfectionism to me as "vanity run amok." The notion was that anyone was crazy to think that they could be a flawless performer, and they would likely drive themselves and others close to them "crazy" in that frustratingly futile pursuit. In this case, my colleague was reflecting on the unhappy outcome of feeling impelled to strive for extreme attainment and control just to feel okay.

In the words of one child psychiatrist, "Perfectionism is the belief that any mistake or flaw, no matter how minor, is unacceptable. For children to overcome this belief, they need to be helped to see the world in less extreme ways."[12] One only child explained the development of her perfectionism this way. "Only children are, by definition, underdogs—a minority of one—and at the same time, they have too much clout and significance: the redemptive power, or so they imagine, to repair what is broken and fill what is empty in their parents' lives. The necessity to rise and shine daily, like a puny sun around which two mighty satellites revolve, nurtures a grandiose and morbid perfectionism."[13] (It also nurtures the only child's *sensitivity to unfairness,* to unequal treatment, that she develops thanks to a message from her parents that sets a double standard she typically resents. She is expected to act grown-up but must remember she is still a child governed by rules that they make and can live above, and that's not fair!)

Perfectionism is a painful cross to bear. By definition, someone who believes perfection is desirable and attainable has committed himself to a series of very debilitating beliefs.

- He can't allow failure.
- He can't take criticism.
- He can't admit mistakes.
- He can't correct mistakes.
- He can't learn from mistakes.
- He can't admit to being wrong.
- He can't admit wronging others.
- He can't apologize for wrongdoing
- He can't make amends for doing wrong.
- He can't accept that life is real and not ideal.
- He can't enjoy doing what he's not accomplished at.
- He can't relax his efforts or rest on his laurels for doing well.
- He can't do something a little wrong without feeling it's all wrong.
- He can't resist controlling those on whom his performance depends.
- He can't escape the constant fear of failing to maintain his flawless record.
- He can't give up stressfully striving to maintain the inhuman standard he has set.
- He can't relieve the stress under which he continually labors without criticizing others.

Parents should discuss the high costs of perfectionism so the only child can see the unhappiness such unrealistic striving brings.

If as a parent you are afflicted by this unhealthy ambition, you might want to review the costs yourself. After all, one common motivation for having a single child is being able to devote all parental attention to the job in order to do it right. And if you are an adult only child in a significant relationship, you might want to ask your partner about all the ways your perfectionism is hard to live with. Or you might get help like the adult only child who married the youngest of five children, a woman "who, he says, allows him to be less than perfect and teases him so that he never loses touch with the fact that he is not perfect and that she doesn't want him to be. All only children need that from time to time."[14] Or as another adult only child put it: "At long last I am now trying to be 'me,' whoever that is. I shall never be perfect, but I think I'm ok."[15] Acceptance of one's human foibles, frailties, and failures is one way to break the hold of perfectionism.

A psychologist who specializes in these matters suggests a way to liberate oneself from this debilitating belief. "'What do I do about perfectionism? Shoot for mediocrity and failure?' Of course not. The key is to learn the difference between the hopeless pursuit of perfection and the satisfying seeking of excellence . . . A piece of advice that I give to all perfectionists and especially to only children is: Lower your high jump bar of life. Others haven't put that bar so high—*you* have, as you have reached for perfection and made real success impossible. When you learn to settle for excellence, however, life will be more satisfying, happier, and more fulfilling, as you clear the bar and then some."[16]

Parents can help the only child avoid the harsh pressures of perfectionism by explaining the difference between being human (which he is) and being ideal (which he is not), and between effort (which he controls) and outcome (which he doesn't). They could say, "Don't place inhuman demands on human performance. Failure to reach an ideal such as perfection is not evidence of failing as a human being. Don't judge your effort by the outcome. A failed outcome (you didn't get what you wanted) does not mean that your effort was a failure (you tried hard and took action.)"

My favorite advice about how to reduce perfectionist tendencies comes from a poet-songwriter, not a psychologist. It is from the Leonard Cohen song, *Anthem.*

"Forget your perfect offering,
There is a crack in everything."

If your only child is an adolescent, share these lyrics with him or her. Then reflect on the good things that can happen when things don't turn out perfectly as planned, about how imperfections make everything uniquely different, and how on close enough examination and viewed from enough different perspectives everything is flawed.

In addition to helping the child learn to choose her ambitions carefully and compassionately, parents must also make sure they are not priming her to accomplish their unfulfilled personal dreams.

FULFILLING PARENTAL DREAMS

The influence of dreams for their child is an area of vulnerability for parents from which a lot of pressure can flow. Two kinds of dreams can amplify the power of parental ambitions: dreams of similarity and dreams of differentness. A *similarity dream* might be: "I wanted my child to be socially involved and have a large circle of friends like I did; but she prefers to spend her time alone instead." Parental disappointment in the girl's solitary path through school may encourage the daughter to feel disappointed in herself: "I'll never be as popular as Mom was or as she wants me to be." A *differentness dream* might be: "I wanted my son to graduate high school and not drop out to work like I did, but that is just what he has done." Parental disappointment at the boy's educational choice may encourage the son to feel disappointed in himself: "I'll never be the student Dad wanted." *Parents need to be sensitive to a child's ambitions that are connected to their dreams, because when the dreams are not realized, their disappointment can have a crushing impact on their only child.*

It can be helpful for parents to take an inventory of their own *dream agendas.* They can ask themselves two questions.

1.   In what ways does it feel very important to me for my child to make the *same* choices as I did growing up?

2. In what ways does it feel very important to me for my child to make *different* choices than I did growing up?

The answers can represent emotionally loaded areas of concern for parents. Knowing them in advance helps keep parents from over-reacting when the child fails to fulfill their dreams. It is also helpful for them to remember that what was of value to them may not be of value to the child, and what may have been a mistake for the parents may not be a mistake for the child. "Just because I regret not playing high school sports doesn't mean that your not playing sports, but doing band instead, isn't a good decision for you."

For the only child, the trap of striving to fulfill unmet parental aspirations is sprung by a sense of obligation to accomplish what they were not able to accomplish for themselves. A daughter may confide: "My mom sacrificed her own desire for a college education by working and saving so I could get mine. That's partly why I went to college instead of starting a full-time job. This degree is not just for me, it's at least as much for her." Or a son may confide: "No matter how hard he tried, my dad never did well in business. It was always hand to mouth. So I wanted to make a lot of money in business not just for myself, but for him to enjoy a sense of financial success through me." *Out of love and loyalty, only children can get caught up in devoting their lives to satisfying the unfulfilled aspirations of their parents.*

To prevent this servitude from developing, parents can make sure they are not pushing the child to satisfy their longings, and they can also make a statement to free the child up. "Just as we created lives to meet our needs and interests, and not our parents', we want you to create a life that works for you, not one designed for us." Then parents need to apply this statement to how their only child charts her path through school.

WHAT ABOUT SCHOOL?

Turning their son or daughter over to a school can be a wrenching experience for parents of an only child. *School is the primary field of play; it is there that a child's ambition to achieve, and the parental ambition for the child, is put to the competitive test.*

Listen to some veteran teachers, and they will often say they are able to identify those students who are only children without having to be told. How do they do this? Usually their judgment is based on individual and social behaviors that seem to differentiate only children from those growing up in multiple-child families. What are these common differences? A few are listed here.

- *At school, only children tend to be lower risk takers and less adventuresome than their peers.* These children are often conservative when it comes to risk taking because they have been brought up by protective parents who train the child to value careful decision making in the interest of personal and social safety. From parents carrying an extra measure of worry about their only child getting hurt, the child often internalizes this worry, exercising caution out in the world. *So the only child is not likely to be the physically or socially daring student a teacher must keep a watchful eye upon, but rather is disinclined to enter into the rough-and-tumble of the playground.*

- *At school, only children tend to have elevated internal standards of academic performance.* Based on high parental expectations and based on their own belief (from being socialized around adults to act adult) that they should be able to operate on an adult level, only children usually are highly motivated to do well. If anything, these children often need help with their intolerance of mistakes and with falling victim to the pressures of perfectionism. *So the only child is not the kind of disinterested or laggard student that a teacher has to push to complete work or perform up to potential.*

- *At school, only children often stand out because of their ease in getting along with adults.* Having grown up with grown-ups at home, only children learn early to mimic adult social poise and speech, and they are not much intimidated by adult authority. Although teachers find these skills can make only children very satisfying to communicate with, this apparent maturity can place these children out of step with peers from multiple-child families, who may envy the only child's capacity to befriend and banter with adults. Other students may even resent the only child for being the "teacher's pet." *So the only child is likely to be a student the teacher enjoys relating to, but may be less than universally popular with peers.*

- *At school, only children tend to follow social rules.* Having been socialized at home to live on the parents' terms in order to please them, only children tend to obey the teacher, who is a surrogate parental authority at school. At the same time, however, because only children peer with adults (their parents), they often assume for themselves equal standing with the teacher. Because they are not intimidated by adult authority, they often feel free to question rules they do not agree with, and they expect a discussion to follow. *So the only child is not likely to break rules or make trouble, but he or she may well be a student unafraid of speaking up to a teacher over some point of disagreement.*

- *At school, only children often raise their hand, waiting to be called on to show what they know, and feel frustrated when someone else is chosen to answer.* Used to occupying center stage at home, only children go from being the one and only in their family to being one of many in the classroom. This change can prove to be a major adjustment, particularly in the early grades when only children must learn to tolerate being given less opportunity to show off what they know and must make do with getting less adult attention. *So the only child is not likely to be the kind of shy student whom a teacher has to encourage to answer an instructional question; but he or she may feel unfairly treated when someone else gets to give the answer first.*

- *At school, only children tend to believe they know the "right" way to do things because they have been living on such self-determined terms at home.* Thus, put in a work group with peers who are together responsible for producing a single project that will be the basis for grading everyone, an only child can feel enormously frustrated, even threatened, when other students won't do the job his or her way. In response, the only child may take on the extra work of taking charge in order to dictate and control the outcome. *So the only child is likely to have a lot to learn about working cooperatively with others on a common task, about making the necessary compromises so that everyone can contribute a valued share.*

Around the issue of grades, there are three things *not* to say to "motivate" your only child.

- "Do your best."
- "Just try your hardest."
- "Work up to your potential."

All that these ill-defined abstract statements do is put the child at the mercy of his own extreme interpretations of what these terms mean; he may often feel bad about his efforts because he could always do better, try harder, demonstrate more potential. Better for parents to specify the lowest level of grade performance they think is okay. "B's are the minimum grades we will accept from you. Fall below that level of performance, and we will provide supervision and support to help you raise your grades back up. As for the maximum grades you can accomplish, that is up to you to determine. Only you can know how high to achieve."

The watchword for parents of an only child when he or she goes to school is "trust": Trust the preparation you have made. Most only children avoid getting into social trouble, come to make a few close friends, stay clear of peer group pressure, and end up doing well academically.

SUMMARY

Not every only child is a high achiever, but most only children are ambitious to achieve because their parents encourage them to do so and the child desires to meet their expectations. From the combination of parental aspirations and the child's own, performance pressures can flow. Grown-up standards of behavior acquired very young by a child who identifies with parents and wants to be treated as their equal often create an unrealistic set of self-expectations in the only child. Treated as a small adult, he believes he should be able to perform at that advanced level, even though he is a child.

Set unreasonably high, the only child's ambition can create undue pressure unless parents help the child set ambitions appropriate to age and ability. It also helps if parents, when their child enters adolescence and when some degree of falling away from traditional ambitions is likely to occur, do not overreact and make a hard situation worse, but provide steady supervision to support a consistent effort instead.

Parents must also be alert to signs of that unhealthy ambition, perfectionism, which can create multiple sources of unhappiness unless they speak up to help the child moderate this unhappy tendency. Parents must also be careful not to burden the child with their unfulfilled ambitions and unrealized dreams. And parents should stay informed but generally relax about school. In most cases, their only child will do fine.

11

RESPONSIBILITY

A Matter of Commitment

The only child tends to be like his parents—conscientious, serious-minded, and responsible. Partly, this is defensive. He doesn't want to be chastised for managing his affairs like a careless child; he wants respect for leading his life like the adults he lives with. He wants to act grown-up, and what is a more powerful sign of being grown-up than taking responsibility? On the problematic side, however, the extent of liability for what happens, the extent of obligations he owes others, particularly his parents, and how actively he worries about what might go wrong, all come with the territory of responsibility. Like his parents, the only child holds himself to be highly accountable, which is why he can often be too serious for his own comfort.

Common injunctions for responsibility that many adult only children seem to live by include:

- "watch yourself,"
- "question yourself,"
- "doubt yourself,"
- "analyze yourself,"
- "understand yourself,"
- "control yourself."

To their detriment, parents can assume unrealistic liability for how their child grows and indulge in excessive worry in an effort to protect their child. The extent of liability they assume and the degree to which they choose to worry are what determine how heavy the weight of their parental responsibility comes to feel. The most telling expression of that heaviness is the seriousness that marks their attitude.

The psychology of resemblance now comes into play: like parent, like child. The more serious the parents, the less lighthearted their only child is likely to feel. By the attitude toward life that they exemplify, they raise an only child who shares that *seriousness about personal responsibility*—one of the most defining characteristics of the adult only child. The only child tends to be much more careful than carefree. So it is in the interest of both parents and only child for the adults to limit liability and to lessen worry so their child learns to do the same.

LIABILITY

Parents who are determined to do all they can to chart and guide a safe passage of growth for their only child have to keep the extent of their actual influence in perspective. Certainly parenting matters, but it is by no means *all* that matters when it comes to directing a child's growth. In my earlier book *Positive Discipline,* I list a number of sources of influence over which parents have little control.

Parents don't control:

- the *culture* into which the child is born or the onslaught of media messages that it sends—the experiences it glamorizes, the ideals it presents, the models it exemplifies, and the motivations it encourages.
- the child's inborn *characteristics*—the temperament, personality, aptitudes, and physical traits that genetic inheritance endows.
- the *choices* the child makes—the personal decisions that ultimately determine what he or she will or will not do.
- the *circumstances* to which a child is exposed away from home— the unfamiliar and challenging situations he or she gets into out in the world.
- the child's *companions* and the pressures they can bring to bear— the opportunities for risk taking, for experimenting with adventure and the forbidden, which peers provide.

- the *chance* events—the play of luck that can favor, spare, or victimize a young person's life.[1]

I go on to suggest:

Since parenting is only one of many influences on a child's development, how your child "turns out" is not all to your credit or to your blame...As a parent, you need realistic humility. You need to say the following to yourself. "I am not all powerful. I am not all knowing. I am not perfect. I cannot fully protect my child any more than I can fully prepare my child. I can be right some of the time, but not all of the time. I can be sensitive to some of my child's needs, but not to all of my child's needs. I cannot always be at my child's side. I can inform my child's choice, but I cannot control that choice. I can be totally committed to my child's welfare, but I cannot totally ensure that welfare even though I wish I could"...What is the extent of parental influence? As a parent, you influence your child, the example you model (who and how you are), the treatment you give (how you choose to act and react with your child), the structure you impose (what you value and allow), and the education you impart (what information and instruction you provide).[2]

The more liability parents assume for their child's actions or whatever befalls him, the heavier the weight of their responsibility will be, and the more likely the child will come to bear that weight himself. To worsen matters, parents can be prone to excessive worry.

WORRY

Parents of an only child tend to be like conservative investors whose first concern is to safeguard their resources, paying close attention to what is happening and what *might* happen to threaten what they value most. Because their entire parenting investment is in a single child, they want to do what they can to keep that son or daughter from harm, using worry to anticipate dangerous possibilities they can avoid or prevent. With all their eggs in one basket, they can't afford to let the basket drop. So it is natural that many only children come out of "childhoods populated with hovering parents."[3]

Because mother and father are usually first-time parents, they tend to carry a double load of anxiety. First, they have normal new parent insecurity in an unfamiliar role. And second, because this is first and last child in one, they don't want to mess up their one chance at parenting by making mistakes. Holding themselves highly accountable, they raise a child who learns to become the same. Just as there are very few laidback and relaxed parents of an only child, this is true for only children themselves. *"Watch your step"* is a guiding principle of only-child growth. An only child can sense this parental anxiety, actually incorporating their fear of his getting hurt or making mistakes into his own decision making. As one only child in counseling put it, "I think the reason I'm so cautious and concerned about avoiding danger and not messing up is because that's how my parents are with me. They are very careful in their parenting, and that's the way I've learned to treat myself."

The only child is a *trial child.* This means he or she is the one on whom mother and father get to try out their parenting skills and develop their parenting strategies, usually for the first time. The only child can feel that as trial child she is on constant trial to prove not her innocence, but her competence—responsibility being the most valued competence of all. Why is responsibility the most valued competence for parents? The answer is that, when it comes to making safe choices without having parents around, it is the child's best protector. The overprotection parents are tempted to provide, however, is often the enemy of the safety they are trying to create.

OVERPROTECTION

Parental worry and protectiveness increases the sense of responsibility for an only child. Parents who are naturally proactive, looking and thinking ahead, keeping an eye out for danger, teach their only child to cautiously and carefully do the same. For example, a mother who sees her four-year-year-old start to scramble up a jungle gym climbs up behind him just in case. She is ready to catch him should he slip and fall. Urgently she issues instructions about keeping his eyes on the bars, going slowly, planting his feet, and holding on with both hands. Now what felt adventurous and fun to the little boy suddenly feels so dangerous and scary that he appeals to his mother to help him down.

That's the problem with protection. Intended to create safety, it can end up eroding confidence and causing alarm. Then the parents achieve the opposite of what they intended. Acting to help the child feel safe, they actually exacerbate his fears.

For example, there's a burglary on the block and for several nights a seven-year-old only child voices concerns to parents about a stranger breaking into their home. In response, to help the child feel safe, parents purchase some protections—a new alarm system, changed locks on the doors, window bars, and some self-defense weaponry should an entry occur. "There," the parents think, "that should help our daughter feel more secure!" Of course, the opposite is true. Now the girl, surrounded by material evidence of impending danger, is more frightened than before.

Come adolescence, parents have to be extremely careful about not disabling the only child with their fears when she is insecure because so many changes and challenges are occurring. Parental worry sends a vote of no confidence in her competency and readiness for more responsibility. It's like telling the teenager, who already has enough growing-up anxieties of her own, "We don't know if you can handle this opportunity; you might get hurt." Better for parents to say: "Let's talk about how you can prepare yourself for this new experience so things go well." Building adolescent confidence with preparedness works better than creating doubt with worry.

A primary responsibility of parents should be to protect the only child from parental fears. For example, refrain from teaching parental fear by acting like the dad at the park who yanked his only child back from petting a stray dog by yelling: "Don't you know you could get bitten doing something like that?" No, the child didn't know, but she does now, and what felt friendly becomes threatening. The parental need to protect is not there only for the child; the adults wish to protect the child from their own fears, and themselves from regret and guilt and sorrow if the child should come to harm. Overprotection causes parents to take excessive responsibility for what might happen, and encourages the child to learn to do the same.

One parent testifies to this temptation.

There is a strong tendency in one-child families for parents to be overprotective. And this overprotectivenss can become a real handicap for an only child, preventing her from developing in a normal way, in a way that grows naturally from experience, from trial and error, and from freedom to learn for herself. Instead of being overprotective, we parents of only children need to give our child the techniques that will enable him to sort things out, the values that will contribute to making sound judgments, and the self-confidence that he needs in order to know that ultimately he will be able to function competently by himself. The problem is that in order for our only children to learn what good decisions are, they have to make some bad ones as well. This is particularly trying for parents of one child to witness because so much is invested in that one individual. *Frightened parents raise frightened children.*[4]

Cautious and anxious children can become protective parents. For example, consider the wife, an only child, and her husband, who grew up with siblings, in disagreement about whether to send their only child to public or private school. She wants to shelter her child in a more controlled private setting while he wants his daughter to learn social confidence through coping with the more complex social realities that public schooling can provide.

Sheltering is a form of protection that parents provide the only child. A familiar example is paying for a private school, for two common reasons:

- To protect the child from real and imagined risks associated with the larger size, laxity of discipline, and social diversity of a public school.
- To accelerate the child's education with the real and imagined benefits of more academic focus and improved preparation.

Whether parents get what they pay for depends on the situation, but the costs of sheltering are frequently included in the price:

- Delaying adolescent growth to independence by imposing a structure that is strictly demanding of social obedience can encourage dependency.

- Limiting experience by restricting social exposure to a larger and more complex social world can reduce social competence.

Parents have to dare to let their only child take risks, accepting that his getting bumps, bruises, and breaks is sometimes the price of learning as he grows. As one mother of an only child described it, preparation builds confidence, while overprotection undercuts it. Parents of an only son or daughter are "all too eager to 'bubble-wrap' their child. Everything is a first time and a last time with one child, and parents can't bear to let anything go wrong... Our minds are full of what-ifs? We fear what we do not know and know that there is much to fear."[5] *Worry is how parents base responsibility on fear.*

Parents of an only child must be brave. They have so much to lose. They fear making the wrong decisions for the child and thus inflicting unintentional harm or exposing her to excessive risk. They fear the child's becoming victim of her own impulsive or unwise decisions. They fear the adverse influence of other children. They fear that chance or circumstance might strike their child down. There is so much to fear and so little they control, it is easy to give in to the tyranny of fear: "We don't how we'd survive if anything happened to our child!" So parents must learn to restrain their fear lest it become contagious to their child. The key to moderating fearful attention with their only child is to learn to distinguish between constructive and destructive worry.

CONSTRUCTIVE VERSUS DESTRUCTIVE WORRY

Constructive worry is responsible. It is *proactive parenting.* Recognizing that a normal part of being a child is acting without first considering the risks, parents try to increase the child's vision of harmful possibilities by saying something like this. "Because we don't want to send you blindly into a new situation you have never experienced, we want you to think about an important question: *What if?* We want to anticipate with you some possible problems that might arise. And then we want you to come up with some plans, just in case any of these difficulties should occur. We are not saying that any of this will happen, but if it did, how would you act to take care of yourself?"

Constructive worry protects the only child from risks in life by preparing her for dealing with what might arise. *By using constructive worry, parents teach their only child to stop and think ahead.* Knowing that this forethought is in place often reduces the amount of anxiety parents feel, and they are able to send their child off into some new experience supported by their confidence and not burdened by their fears.

Destructive worry can lead to *compulsive overparenting,* in which parents drive themselves and their only child crazy with excessive control. Parents can *chain-worry:* "If you flunk this class, then maybe you'll flunk others, then maybe you'll drop out of school, and then maybe you'll end up living on the street!" Parents can ask crazy questions (questions for which there are no answers): "How do you know for sure you won't get hit by a drunk driver and get killed?" Parents can *obsessively control:* "You're not going out unless you check in with us by phone every half hour." Compulsive overparenting invokes strategies for safety that only worsen parental fears.

If parents ever find themselves crossing the line that separates constructive from destructive worry, they can reduce the tendency to compulsively overparent by:

- trying to confine their worries to the near future, and not chain worry into a far-distant time;
- trying to interrupt the flow of crazy questions by only allowing those for which sensible answers exist;
- and trying to let go of what cannot realistically be controlled.

Two researchers on only children noted: "Our observation of the daily lives of only children and their parents convinces us that caution is often carried to the point where it defeats its own purpose . . . Confining a child will not prevent worry any more than it will teach him to take care of himself. On the contrary, the only way to stop worrying is, within reason, to make a child responsible for his own actions. Once you find that you can trust him, your troubles are over."[6] *Evidence of responsibility in the only child is what builds parental trust, and most only children learn responsibility well.*

If you are an adult only child who finds yourself more prone to worry than you would like, conjuring up fearful possibilities that most often do not occur, understand that you likely absorbed these anxieties from your parents who had too many anxieties of their own. Then consider separating constructive from destructive worry, using the former to think ahead (what you are probably good at) and letting go those which are too far removed, which you know are irrational, or over which you have no control (what you need to learn).

Anticipate that *change* may be especially anxiety provoking. Going from a known to an unknown situation requires attention to the new circumstances, experience, or relationship before it can become comfortable, familiar, and manageable. Just as your parents were anxious about change in your life because of the risks it could bring, you may have learned to be the same. If so, don't allow the fear of change to back you off from pursuing what you want. Instead, ask yourself: *What would I choose to do if I were not afraid?* Then see if you can't use constructive worry to prepare a path toward this objective.

If you are parents who are "worried sick" about your only child as she graduates from the security of your care and is taking off into the risky world of independent living far away, for your own sanity, place your trust in the responsibility that you have taught her. That good preparation, along with your child's good sense, will usually provide the protection she needs. And rest assured: should your only child get into trouble, she will give you a call as she grapples with the challenges of living on her own.

INDEPENDENCE

One dimension of responsibility is independence. A writer observes, "Responsibility for oneself is a form of independence . . . It is quite possible that only children develop a sense of self-reliance sooner and more deeply than others. When parents have only one child, especially if they are older, they may consciously foster a spirit of independence."[7] As one only child put it: "'I have absolutely no regrets about being an only child. I liked the responsibility and independence of it . . . My parents gave me a lot of independence quite early.'"[8] There's a lot of confidence and self-esteem that responsible independence brings.

Why do only children tend to develop a strong sense of responsibility so young? Because the more they identify with adults, the more like an adult they act, the more like an adult they are treated. In the words of one grown only child: "To me, being responsible meant acting grown-up just like my parents. Doing the kinds of things for myself they did for themselves. Simple things. Cleaning up after myself. Keeping promises to them like they kept promises to me. Finishing what I started. Giving help where I could. That's how my parents were, so that's how I tried to be." *A heightened sense of responsibility just seems to come with the territory of being an only child.* And with this strength can come a liability.

It is easy for parents to forget that their only son or daughter, though socially mature, is still a child in need of the unrestricted, thoughtless, carefree freedom that is part of a healthy growing up. *Freedom from adult responsibility* is a playful side of what a childhood is about. Giving oneself over to fun and games and adventure without having to worry about acting mature like parents allows the boy or girl to develop his or her childish side. Therefore, while still valuing the adultlike qualities of their only child, parents can encourage this important freedom from responsibility by adequately socializing him with other children of the same age. The only child cannot learn to act his or her age by associating with adults. The boy or girl must be given the opportunity to interact with peers. This said, only child teenagers can be so deeply imbued with a sense of responsibility (and sense of rectitude) that they won't join in impulsive adventures of the adolescent age. Just as they tend not to rebel very strongly against parents, they tend to be too responsibly conservative to run wild with friends. They are calculators when it comes to making decisions, delaying choice to consider consequences, weighing the worth of effort against the value of outcome, figuring the likelihood that an objective can be gained. *How to balance freedom from and freedom for responsibility is one of the most complicated tasks of parenting an only child* because it is so tempting for the only child to want older responsibility and for parents to grant it. This "little adult" is a very responsible child, but the outcome is alloyed: a mixture of pride in and pressure from all this grown-up accomplishment. Additionally complicating responsibility is an associated set of demands: obligation to parents.

OBLIGATION TO PARENTS

A common outcome of being raised as an only child is a significant sense of responsibility to and for the parents, partly from having received so much from parents and partly because there are no siblings with whom to share parental care. "Most only children feel a strong sense of obligation to care for their parents. Sometimes it comes from genuine devotion. Sometimes it is a continuation of a lifetime of parental expectations. Most of the time, it is a combination of both."[9]

When parents graduate a late adolescent from their care into adult independence, responsibility to and for each other can be a tie that bonds or a tie that binds, depending on how obligatory it feels. "Please call and see us when you want to, not because you feel you should" encourages contact based on the desire to care and share. Obligation restricts freedom of choice and can engender guilt. Because most only children grow up with a heavy sense of obligatory responsibility to parents, it behooves parents to release the young person from this sense of duty in order to open up freedom for friendship in the years ahead.

To keep the terms of obligation from becoming unduly oppressive, parents might want to consider omitting the words "should" and "ought" when discussing what they want and don't want to happen. (The only child already overuses these words for himself out of rectitude, as described in chapter 9.) For both parents and the only child, a sense of mutual obligation is deeply ingrained, and neither needs to carry any more. There's danger here. *If they invoke obligation often enough, parents can actually end up alienating the affection of the child they love.*

Therefore, discuss with your only child four questions about obligation that, particularly when grown, she will have to answer for herself to determine what is owed to the parents who have given her so much.

- *Communication:* How much should she confide in you? How much should she tell to keep you currently informed?
- *Contact:* How often should she see you and be a visiting presence in your life?

- *Celebration:* How regularly should she mark special occasions and holidays with you?
- *Caretaking:* How much support should she provide for you, particularly in your times of physical needs, and ultimately in the years of decline, disease, disability, and dying?

Remember, if you are divorced, you have *doubled the amount of obligation* the only child must manage. Now she must balance her contribution to you and your ex, and she must cope with your competing wants and needs when you both want to have her in your separate lives at the same time.

I encourage parents to try and set limits on these contributions from the child to relieve the pressure of obligation she will naturally feel. The high school years are a good time to dialogue with her about this, before she graduates and separates more from home. Should she fail to meet her sense of obligation, guilt is the price she will pay: "I can never do enough for my parents!"

THE BURDEN OF GUILT

Two researchers concluded that, "the pressure of all the expectations, with only you to achieve them, creates a strong sense of obligation in many aspects of only children's lives. This very easily translates into guilt. One of the enduring impressions left with us is that guilt is an indelible part of the only-child condition . . . 'Never enough' is the resonant phrase. However hard they tried, only children rarely felt they had achieved as much as was expected of them. And what's the result of all this? Only children tend to be very hard on themselves. Others' high expectations of them are nothing to what they expect of themselves. The hardest taskmaster for the only child is himself."[10]

The greatest vulnerability from the obligation parents and their only child feel is guilt for failing to do their duty to each other. The more that mutual obligation governs their relationship ("I must do well to make my parents proud"; "We must do everything we can to make our child happy"), the more susceptible to guilt everyone is. At worst, enthroning obligation dictates a set of terms that are oppressive to live with for everyone.

A side vulnerability for parents and only child is a susceptibility to having their guilt from obligation used for manipulative gain. Thus the only child, thwarted by parental refusal of what he or she wants, angrily charges; "You never let me have anything; you just don't love me, and I don't love you!" and begins to cry. Can parents hold withstand such cruel beliefs and obvious suffering? If not, if they give in to this emotional extortion and allow the child to get his way, their susceptibility to guilt will be played upon to destructive effect.

The same is true when parents, to get their adolescent only child to stay home with them instead of going out to socialize with friends, pull the strings of guilt to get their way. "You never spend any time with us. You treat us like we just don't matter to you anymore. But if that's the way you feel, then just go out and have a good time. We'll stay home by ourselves. Alone." Now both parents look hurt in order to drive home their implied statement of suffering. Is the child going to be able to pull away? The child will not do so without feeling torn and hurt and angry.

The sense of responsibility and the sense of obligation are not the same, although the second can easily develop from the first, as it often does in only-child families. *Responsibility has to do with accountability,* making independent decisions and agreeing to cope with the consequences, for good or ill. *Obligation has to do with indebtedness,* honoring what is owed to others and feeling the need to pay them back.

Because parents and their only child are often grateful for what each has received from the other, a sense of mutual indebtedness can develop early in their family relationship. "It isn't just love that keeps me and my parents so close. It's a sense of duty. I feel like I owe them so much, and they feel the same way about me."

The child, for example, may resolve: "Since I am the one and only child they have, I *should:*

- turn out well,
- make them proud,
- make them happy,
- carry on the family line,
- remain the center of their world,
- repay them for all they have invested,

- take care of them when they are sick or old,
- make sure holidays and special occasions go well,
- and keep in contact after leaving home so they don't get lonely."

On their side, parents may have their own set of resolves: "Since this is the one and only child we have, we *should:*

- make our child happy,
- help our child to succeed,
- sacrifice for our child to get ahead,
- include our child in our adult world,
- notice when anything is going wrong,
- protect our child from possible dangers,
- avoid making mistakes that would harm our child,
- and support our child's development in every way we can."

Although parents with multiple children might subscribe to many of these statements, they are not likely to do so with as much sense of obligation as parents with an only child. In some only-child families, the sense of duty can seem almost contractual: *Parents should provide and protect, and the only child should please and perform.* Of course, obligatory responsibility does have its positive side. Most only children feel they should take themselves seriously, act conscientiously, and do any task to the best of their ability. Like their mother and father who try very hard, most only children want to do their level best.

SUMMARY

In addition to carrying the heavy burden of responsibility to live up to parental expectations of performance and to strive to emulate adult behavior, the only child must deal with four other issues associated with responsibility: seriousness, worry, obligation, and guilt.

Because parents take their role so seriously when raising their first and last child in one, the only child takes his own role that way, too, a sense of seriousness about personal responsibility being one of the psychological hallmarks of the adult only child. And just as parents are prone to worry about how their only child is going to do and what could happen to him, the only child is often prone to worry, too. He anticipates possible danger, he proceeds with caution in areas where he lacks confidence, he is generally conservative when it comes to risk taking, and he wants to act as responsibly as he can. Like his parents, he needs to learn to discriminate between constructive worry (thinking ahead) and destructive worry (imagining the worst).

Obligation to parents is usually a major part of an only child's responsibility, particularly after he leaves their care, one that he and they need to relax when he becomes an adult if they are to enjoy friendship during his grown-up years. At worst, the only child can be ruled by guilt from not living up to parental expectations and from failing to meet his obligation to those who have given him so much. By eliminating the words "should" and "ought" from their discussions with the child, parents can go a long way toward reducing his natural susceptibility to guilt.

12

POSSESSIVENESS

A Matter of Ownership

The only child is very self-possessed. Without siblings to contest the decisions she makes, to interfere with the direction she takes, or to curtail the definition she develops, the only child becomes her own creation. From this primary sense of belonging, a sense of ownership grows. She is her own person. And that ownership entitles her to be in charge of her life and to lead it independently, with a stronger individual inclination than a communal one. On the problematic side, however, sharing ownership of what and who matters to her and collaborating for joint benefit can all be difficult to do. Possessiveness can make sharing difficult when one is used to unilateral decision making. Jealousy is hard to avoid when sharing a loved one's love with others. And possessing sufficient private space, both physical and psychological, is a condition for any adult attachment.

Being self-possessed means the only child takes ownership control of how he defines and directs himself. He doesn't want other people telling him what to think, how to act, or who to be. By making his own decisions, he "owns" his life. By taking charge of it he claims responsibility. How did he get this way? "It may be that the less traditional upbringing of the only child makes him or her more comfortable with individuality. An only child must find his own path, after all, not follow in advance of or behind a sibling. Emancipated to some degree from tradition and authority, the only child may personify . . . personal independence."[1]

Growing up within the unavoidable constraints of family and the undeniable influence of parents, he still becomes very much his own person because of the way his capacities are nurtured, his wants are catered to, and his accomplishments are doted on. In addition, he is free from having to adjust or accommodate to any siblings who have competing wants of their own, who he has to move over for, step aside for, defer to, share with, contest against, compare to, or otherwise put up with. His precious birthright is created through a combination of full parental indulgence and the absence of rivals.

Without sibling competition, he explores, defines, and occupies the entire unmapped territory of what it means to be the only child in his family. To do this, he has an enormous amount of time alone to do with himself what he wants for himself without anyone else dictating that determination for him. He is given the power to creatively nurture his own definition to a degree that children in larger households are generally not.

In a word, by late childhood, he has gotten accustomed to exercising an enormous amount of *self-control* in his life. Control over what?

- *Control of self-interest:* He got to pursue what mattered to him.
- *Control of the outcome from his efforts:* He got to enjoy all the fruits of his labor.
- *Control of the destiny he wanted to work toward:* He got to set his own course and goals.

What he generally did *not* get was much experience being a joiner or a collaborator. He learned more about being a solo operator used to making unilateral decisions, and he learned to limit social conformity to preserve his own individuality. He didn't like being interfered with or being interrupted when doing "his thing," and was not inclined to compromise what he cared about to please others. Given the choice between being a leader or a follower, he would prefer leading because then at least he could influence an outcome that came closer to fitting his self-interest. Otherwise, given a choice between playing an individual or a team sport, for example, depending on himself was more appealing than depending on teammates. Owning the investment, direction, and credit for his efforts comes to characterize the only child who is truly *self-possessed.*

In relationship with a partner, this characteristic can be misunderstood, the other person resenting the adult only child's dominating ways, calling them "selfish and controlling." But what is really going on with the only child is not some power-hungry need to run the partner's life, but a dedicated insistence on continuing to live on the only child's own self-possessed terms, terms that can sometimes make sharing in a relationship unappealing.

SHARING

One popular image of the only child is someone who, lacking competition from siblings and benefiting from all that parents have to give, is disinclined to share what is valued. This image is partly false and partly true. It is false because when possessing so much materially that sharing is a small sacrifice, when having something worth sharing affirms self-worth, or when the role of sharer is socially empowering, the only child likes to share and does it willingly and well. Having money to go to a movie with friends, for example, the only child may happily buy refreshments for her companions.

Where this ease of sharing tends to become more difficult is with possessions of personal value, a collection of toys, for example, that the only child wants kept in a particular order, on immaculate display, and left untouched. Remember, this is a child with no siblings to disturb her belongings, siblings who, with or without her permission, would play with her things. *A strong sense of ownership—of the right to lead one's life and to control the use of one's belongings—comes with being an only child.*

For the only child, *possessions can be personal* because she tends to identify with the important ones. They don't just "belong" to her; they are an expression of her being, an extension of her, a part of how she defines herself, a part of who she is. More than children with siblings, the only child is prone to being possessed by her possessions, both growing up and as an adult. A damaged object can produce a hurt person. "My dolls are not mine, they are *me!*," one young only child told her parents to explain why she wanted to break up with a friend who had broken a beloved doll. Some good advice for parents in this situation is to understand how sharing prized possessions can be hard to do. "An only child who learns to share when other children come to play may feel less resentful and happier to oblige—knowing that it's for a short while! One problem which often arises when other children come to play . . . is a special toy which has enormous significance to a particular child and there is no way she is going to share it under any circumstance. In this case it's better to put the toy safely away until the visit is over. As children grow older and are more used to sharing they don't seem to be quite so affected by special toys. In fact, they are probably eager to show them off and play with them cooperatively."[2] When still young, however, the only child usually enjoys her freedom from the need to share: "I never have to wait my turn at all. It's always my turn because I'm an only child."[3]

Sharing must be learned. And sometimes the process can be painful, as it was for the only child in high school who wanted her parents to host a foreign exchange student for a year. The child expected the newcomer would be both a fellow student and close companion to enjoy. And at first the student was, until the parents found much to admire in this guest that was lacking in their child, who then felt threatened both by the comparisons made and by the loss of parental attention now directed elsewhere. Instead of turning out to be some kind of idealized sibling, this student from another country felt like a real rival, and the only child did not enjoy sharing the home stage.

When an only child has not learned much by way of sharing growing up, about the small inconveniences and frustrations thereof, then the early phase of an adult partnership can be challenging indeed. Parents may have neglected preparation for this part of the child's future. One writer observes, "Like everyone who gets married, only children have to make adjustments. It may be hard, for instance, for an independent only child to share a bedroom and bureau."[4]

Marriage means sharing, combining two separate self-interests to create a common one both partners are committed to support. Immediately, three sets of competing interests are set up in consequence of this two-party relationship: there is a "me," a "you," and an "us," each in need of satisfaction. So, over the course of marriage, the question often arises: Whose needs come first—mine, yours, or ours? And at what expense for you, for me, for us?

The only child who grows up not having to accommodate to the needs of siblings can find supporting the common needs of a partnership challenging indeed. Consider just a few of the sharing requirements that must now be met: scheduling time together and apart, organizing living space, spending money, making social commitments, creating joint interests, setting goals for the future, and allocating household responsibilities.

As explained in chapter 8, one reason only children don't like to share is the potential for conflict that establishing a common interest and maintaining a working collaboration can create. Two researchers note, "Inexperience of sibling conflict means that they are often not comfortable with conflict in general."[5] Just consider a few of the sharing questions created by cooperation that can lead to conflict. Finding the answers can be as divisive for the young only child sharing cabin space with fellow campers in the summer as for the freshman sharing space with a roommate in college. In either case, the people in the relationship have to decide:

- Who goes first?
- Who gets most?
- Who does what?
- Who knows best?
- Who gets to decide?
- What is equitable and fair?
- Whose way is the right way?

In adolescent and adult attachments, individual freedom must be given up for the sake of the relationship, and finding answers to these questions is how this giving up is done. Of all these questions, the *fair-share question* can be the most sticky for the only child who wants to be treated equitably and justly and not be taken advantage of, either by doing too much of the work or by not receiving enough of the benefits or credit. This question is less upsetting to siblings who, while they dislike it no less, expect inequity, exploitation, unfairness, and injustice in their continuing rivalry with one another. What they accept as an inevitable and unhappy part of their intermittent competition, the inexperienced only child can find intolerable.

Another definition of sharing is "giving up," and for the only child who is used to operating independently, sacrificing traditional autonomy means giving up the degree of self-control that came with his "bachelor freedom." Now marriage requires the only child to live as part of a team. "Living with someone is about being close to an individual of equivalent power (that is, a peer, as distinct from a parent). And it is the absence of that experience that is almost the very definition of only children... When it comes to sharing they are very late starters in the game of cohabitation."[6]

As mentioned, only children often prefer being solo operators to the complexity and vulnerability of interdependence with others. One only-child writer observes, "The only child spends a lot of time alone... At its best, being an only child can enhance the ability to work independently, to use your own initiative, to draw your own conclusions and solve your own problems."[7] In general, collaboration and teamwork are not the only child's preferred way of operating. She would rather do it herself, depend on her own direction, and make independent decisions; she does not like having to divide up responsibility and share credit for accomplishments.

So adult partnership can pose an initial challenge. Assuming the adult only child is making a full-faith effort to learn how to share, however, the spouse needs to be patient with this adjustment. Since sharing skills were not acquired growing up, for a partnership or marriage to work they must be learned later.

Foreseeing this adult adjustment, parents can provide some preparation for the child if they choose. In multiple ways parents can *encourage a variety of social membership experiences* in which sharing skills such as tolerance, negotiation, compromise, concession, self-sacrifice, and taking turns can be practiced as part of the process of getting along. So look for ways to enroll your child in:

- social circles
- shared interest activities
- volunteer service projects
- student partnerships

- team sports
- overnight camps
- part-time or summer jobs
- collaborative work projects
- spontaneous play with groups of friends
- visiting, even traveling, with friends who have siblings

If the child objects because group involvement feels uncongenial and uncomfortable, explain that your job as parents is to prepare him for adulthood, one important part of which is learning to manage the complexity of group membership and all the different kinds of sharing that entails. Most only children prefer one-to-one relationships to the one-among-others kind. They prefer serious individual companionship to casual group play partly because of their possessiveness. They want a best friend to be exclusively committed, and will sometimes feel betrayed when that person socially branches out. Becoming grown-up, conditions of attachment can remain the same, like the adult only child who wanted his wife to give up time with her girl friends because that was now competing with married time with him. *From extreme possessiveness, jealousy can grow.*

JEALOUSY

"Growing up as one of several children in a family is a complex business. Along with companionship, there may be fierce animosities. Along with love and loyalty, there may be jealousy and feelings of rejection."[8] With siblings come rivalry, competition, and conflict, all of which the only child and parents are usually happy to do without. Being in full possession of parental attention and approval, with no one else to claim or contest a share, the only child has no grounds for jealousy in the family, so that is one problem the only child is spared, except the problem is usually not avoided, just *deferred.* Come adulthood and a significant attachment or marriage, for the first time the only child has to share a loved one with others. Now the rivalry issue arises: "You spend time with them you could spend with me!" Now the jealousy issue arises: "You love them more than me!" Of course, for the only child, possessiveness does not simply pertain to material possessions, but to parents as well, and a sense of entitlement to all the love and care they have to give. This possessiveness of loved ones can carry over to best friendships growing up and to significant attachments when adult.

One of the significant social adjustments in life is to grow from the sense of being the only one that needs attending to, to being one of several or many who must compete and be content receiving a partial share of available resources and benefits. Siblings usually learn to do this in their families; only children often do not.

According to one writer, "The arrival of a new baby brother or sister into a household inevitably prompts what the experts call 'dethronement,' and just as inevitably results in feelings of insecurity."[9] The term "dethronement" is a significant one because it implies the *ruling power* of the first child in the family before successors arrive. The queen or king only child never has to relinquish this ruling power to a sibling and so by right of standing comes to believe that all good things from loved ones in the family should come to him. First considered, first in line, and first served is mostly how it is.

Dethronement creates a degree of deprivation of parental affection for the eldest (once the "only") child. Without a sibling, the only child feels no insecurity from having to compete for parental attachment or attention. At the same time, she is given no preparation for sharing a loved one's attachment or attention when, with an adult partner in later years, she has to share that person's love with friends, extended family, and maybe even with that partner's children from a previous relationship or marriage. Used to being the only loved one in a primary relationship, the only child now becomes one of a matrix of loved ones in the partner's life, and from this insecurity, jealousy can be created.

Of course, possessiveness is not just an only-child problem, it can also trouble parents who do not want to socially share the only child with her friends when she is young, telling her, "We can have more fun, just the three of us." Then, when she becomes seriously committed to a young man in her early twenties, all they can do is cast doubt and disapprove because they are jealous of this attachment, fearful that this new relationship will count more for her than the old one with them. They may complain that he is not "good enough." Now the only child can explain to parents how love of partner and love of parents are not the same and so do not detract from one another and affirm that she has room in her heart for everyone.

By being extremely possessive, parents can unintentionally encourage two unhappy outcomes with their child. First, the child may create distance in, or even sever, the relationship with parents to get the freedom or independence he feels he needs. And second, by their example, they can encourage extreme possessiveness in the child that he will bring to adult attachments of his own.

If jealousy is one outgrowth of possessiveness, not wanting to share primary attachments, the need for adequate privacy is another. Possessive of her privacy, the only child wants to put limits on how much she shares of her physical and psychological space.

PRIVACY

One only child described resorting to secrecy to maintain sufficient privacy from parents who watched her so closely and knew her so well. "'The biggest disadvantage to me about being an only child is that I don't always want to talk to my mom and dad,' she says. 'There are things I don't want them to know. I like to be a little secretive about things, but sometimes when you're an only child that's impossible. They want to know what you're doing all the time.'"[10] It is because only children are under such close parental scrutiny, are expected to share of themselves so much, that they learn to become deliberately secretive with parents in ways multiples would not; siblings are able to distract parental concern from one to another and create relief from parental interest or attention. The more probing and invasive parents act, the more secretive the only child can become, the more her need for privacy of inner experience and for separation of personal space.

This may be related to a principle of human intimacy: the closer people grow, the more important adequate separation becomes, so neither party feels engulfed or suffocated by the other and the sense of individuality is not lost. The desire for a lot of closeness, which the only child enjoys with parents, is always counterbalanced, particularly in adolescence, by the fear of having too much.

The only child is in a peculiar position when it comes to private space. Usually there is adequate physical space for privacy, a bedroom for example. But what is missing is adequate psychological space, the freedom to escape parental notice and understanding. As one adult only child explained it: "I need my own space, and people don't always understand that... I like my privacy. I found sharing rooms at college with four other girls very difficult... My room is my cocoon when I live with people. I'll retire and hide away just to get my own space."[11] Researchers have explained the only child's need for adequate personal space this way:

> The need for space is straightforward to describe. It also appears fairly simple in its origins. Space in the shape of their own room, or sufficient rooms around the home to do what they want when they want, is what most only children are brought up with in the absence of any sibling competition. So they are used to having that space as a matter of course, without having to compete for it in any way... If the need for space were confined to the physical it would not be too much of a problem, because there are usually practical ways of dealing with it. But the need for space extends to emotional space also. What do we mean by emotional space? It's the need that the only child expresses in keeping bits of himself private; the reluctance to open up; the unwillingness to trust people with his innermost thoughts..."We're very private people. I think you'll find only children keep ourselves to ourselves much more."... This tendency to be secretive may exacerbate the problems with sharing.[12]

Having grown up with parents who wanted to know everything, only children can become very protective of their personal privacy, even secretively so, to keep from having to share more of themselves then they want others to know. Particularly as the only child begins the journey into adolescence, usually by middle school, parents need to distinguish between what they *need* to know about the child and what they *would like* to know. For example, they *need to know* the social whereabouts of the teenager as she spends more time away from home and out in the world. This is different from what they *would like to know* about what she and her best friend have been talking about for so long on the phone. In the first case, parents *rightfully ex-*

pect to be kept informed, in the second they must learn to live in more ignorance, *respectfully tolerating* the teenager's increasing need for privacy. As for a partner of an adult only child, he or she should expect and respect that person's need for time alone and space (both physical and psychological) for personal privacy.

SUMMARY

From being focused on so powerfully by parents, most only children become self-possessed, developing a strong commitment to maintain their individuality. Center of parental attention, they become center of their own.

In addition, possessiveness creates other issues that the only child must usually address: ownership, sharing, jealousy, and privacy. When it comes to ownership, possessions can feel like an extension of the child, to be looked after with comparable care. Unused to sharing with siblings, many cooperative skills normally learned growing up may be deferred until an adult partnership, when the capacities for tolerance, negotiation, compromise, concession, self-sacrifice, and taking turns are learned.

Possessing all parental love and attention, the only child is normally possessive in best friendships growing up and in adult partnerships later on, and is prone to jealousy when attachments must be shared. The only child can be extremely possessive about the preservation of physical and psychological sanctuary, prizing sufficient separate space, time alone, and personal privacy. This last even extends to secrecy, the means the only child uses to keep the parents who know him so well from finding out *all* about him, for independence' sake.

To a significant degree, ownership, sharing, jealousy, and privacy remain active issues for the adult only child to contend with.

13

APPROVAL

A Matter of Pleasing

The only child knows how to win the approval of parents and other adults, using skills that will help her to make her way in a world ruled by established powers that be. A compliment frequently given to parents of an only child is "She's so good with adults!" In addition, by courting and receiving approval, the only child receives praise that causes her to feel affirmed and empowered. On the problematic side, however, she can equate a lack of approval with a lack of love and so develop a heightened need for approval from authorities and an adult partner. She can also overestimate her capacities and have an extremely low tolerance for disappointment and the disapproval of others. In this regard, adolescence can be a particularly trying time for the only child, because a lot of her oppositional growth during this period of transformation will be displeasing to parents.

The responsibility to please parents comes with being an only child who knows she alone provides all the child-raising satisfaction they will get. As she receives their total investment of parental care, the only child usually feels impelled to give a high-performance return by doing well for the parents, by reflecting well on them, by bringing positive recognition to the family and the good parenting they provide. In the words of one adult only child: "I think one feels obliged to please these parents; you're all they have."[1]

For doing all this, she wants their approval to signify that she has succeeded in pleasing them. This approval then acts like a mirror in which the only child sees herself reflected. "Mirror, mirror, on the wall, who's the fairest of them all?" asks the Queen in *Snow White*. When an only child asks this question of the image reflected in parental eyes, the answer is often a resounding "Me!" From the approval parents routinely give, the only child tends to develop a very positive self-image.

Consequently, only children often tend to:

- consider themselves *capable* and feel confident *pursuing ambitious goals;*
- consider themselves *intelligent* and feel comfortable *expressing their opinions;*
- consider themselves *valuable* and insist on *being treated well.*

"Please the parents" is a guiding principle of the only child's growth because, particularly when he is very young, their expression of approval feels like love, while their disapproval can feel like a loss of love. Parents need to help the child understand that neither conclusion is so.

DISTINGUISHING BETWEEN LOVE AND APPROVAL

Although parental approval can feel like love, and parental love can amplify the power of their approval, parents must help the little boy or girl understand that love and approval are *not* the same. To do so, parents can contrast these two responses—love and approval—so the child can understand the constant nature of the first and the conditional nature of the second.

To clarify this distinction, they can explain how *love is unconditional and abiding.* It represents a *commitment* of devotion that is unwavering and will not be broken. It is a *given.* "We love you because of who you *are*, and we always will." Then they can explain how *approval is conditional and temporary.* It represents an *evaluation* of the degree to which the child, at a given moment in time, is acting in accord with what the parents value or desire. It is *earned.* "We approve of how you *do* when you act as we ask or perform something well." *Approval doesn't prove love any more than love guarantees approval.* The two are independent and need to be kept that way. The child needs the security that comes from understanding that parental disapproval does not connote any loss of parental love.

An adult only child, having grown up so closely attached to parents—bathed in the unconditional acceptance, priority concern, and total focus of their parental love—can find it hard to settle for less than this unconditional love when it comes time to choose a partner. One adult only child poignantly wrote about the adjustment that he had to make. "I had misguidedly imagined marriage as an extension of the loving triangle in which I had grown up, only a four-legged triangle is impossible to shape. One afternoon [my partner] said to me, 'I'm not going to love you unconditionally. I'm not your parents.' Is only parents' love unconditional? I wondered. I wonder still. It is the bittersweet lament of the only child who has been loved only too well."[2] *The adult only child must accept that no partner, no matter how loving, will ever provide the extreme degree of unalloyed admiration, attention, and interest in him that his parents provided.*

The writer's question goes to the heart of the matter. The answer is yes. *Parental love is unconditional.* The child is nurtured in it from birth or adoption. Romantically developed in young adulthood or later, *partner love is conditional.* It is based on terms of *commitment* like marital vows that both agree to. While partners may divorce this commitment to each other when a certain term or condition—faithfulness, for example—ceases to be met, parents, even through the violations and offenses of adolescence, do not typically divorce their child.

Used to exclusive, uncontested, unconditional parental love, the only child to some degree is likely to expect from a partner the same regard he received from his parents. Thus I find, in counseling couples, that an adult only child expects love from a partner to be unconditional; he believes the other should love him independently of how he acts. Then comes the revelation: Adult partnerships are conditional. And when the only-child adult does not meet those conditions, when, for example, standards of equity, support, trust, safety, or loyalty are violated, his partner's commitment may waver and can be thrown open to question: "You can't treat me this way if you want our marriage to continue!" *For the sake of making and keeping a significant adult partnership, the adult only child must learn that unconditional love is what he was given by his parents, but conditional committed love is the best an adult partner can provide.* With parents he was accepted however he acted; with a partner he will be held to stricter account, and he must make a greater effort.

THE LEGACY OF PLEASING

Adult only children tend to remain seekers of approval. They continue to want to please the powers that be, whether a friend, a partner, a coworker, a boss, or salient others. Typically, the adult only children I have seen have a heightened need

- To look and perform well,
- To make a good impression,
- To be generally well thought of,
- To be respected and looked up to,
- To have a positive social reputation.

They definitely seem to have a lower tolerance for any of the following:

- Disappointment
- Criticism
- Correction
- Rejection
- Anger
- Blame
- Teasing
- Sarcasm.

Having acquired grown-up verbal and social skills early by interacting with parents, the adult only child is usually very skilled at pleasing significant authorities as he makes his way through the world, assiduously working for a "good evaluation" wherever he goes. Although he may have a thin skin when it comes to receiving any expressions of dissatisfaction or disapproval, he is well practiced and confident in his communication with authorities, and this usually serves him well.

In a romantic partnership, however, his need for approval can sometimes be hard to satisfy. For example, if he hadn't worked so hard to please his parents and been so well recognized for his efforts, he wouldn't have such a great need to please his partner now. Consider, for example, the adult only child who marries a woman from a large family of siblings, where more competitive attention came from one another than did praise from parents, who probably had their hands full just providing them with the basics. So the only child marries a nondemonstrative woman who sees no need to give or receive much praise or appreciation. "Didn't you like how I reorganized the shelves?" asks the only child. She replies, "If I didn't like the way you did it, I would let you know." And when he says he would like to be regularly assured of her affections, as his parents continually did with him, she explains matter-of-factly: "If I didn't love you, I wouldn't have married you." So in this relationship, you have a praise-hungry only child married to a loving woman who sees little need to exchange praise. This is a hard adjustment for an only child from a family in which pleasing one another and being told one is pleasing has been a routine part of the affirmation of daily life. After receiving so much approval from parents while he was growing up, the only child tends to have a heightened need for it from an adult partner later on, and that partner's disapproval is amplified accordingly.

For parents raising an only child, it is good to give praise, but to do so in moderation so the child does not become dependent on a diet of excessive approval. More important is that the child does not develop a distorted image of his value, capacity, or potential when smitten parents rave, "Amazing!" "You're wonderful!" "You can do anything!" What the child does not realize is that this may be the voice of infatuation or wish fulfillment speaking. The child's image is in danger of becoming *distorted* through the eyes of parents who sincerely believe, or want to believe, that their one and only child's ordinary accomplishments are a miracle of exceptional achievement. Without another child to whom they can compare their first, parents occasionally overreact and lose realistic perspective. As was explained to me by a client years ago: *"Nobody who has an only child believes they have just an average child."* That statement is probably correct. Also true is that few only children start out life being willing to consider themselves only average. One expert on the subject counsels parents to "encourage modesty. Achievements should always be acknowledged and praised, but it isn't a good idea to let the child think she is some sort of a genius."[3]

PROBLEMS WITH OVERPRAISING

What one mother and writer refers to as "overpraising"[4] can distort the child's self-perception. It is easy for parents of an only child to indulge in it, and it contributes to a sense of exceptionality and grandiosity that will later let him down when he turns out to be an average person like most everyone else. This is not to say "Don't praise your child," only do it wisely. *Overpraise from parents can result in overappraisal by the child.*

Consider two models for giving praise, the *esteem booster model* and the *educational feedback model.* The booster model pumps up the only child with superlatives, magnifying the significance of small accomplishments, creating the impression of superiority for the child who can't resist becoming a believer in his own reviews. Enthusiastic parents exclaim, "Nobody could have done it better! If you can do this well now, nothing can hold you back in the future! This just goes to show how talented you are!" Well-intentioned parents, meaning to flood the child with good feelings about herself, provide a nonstop flow of compliments to celebrate her growth at every small step of the way. Although this acclaim is affirming, it has the drawback of deluding the child into believing she is more exceptionally able than she actually is and increases the pressure to perform at an even higher level.

On balance, it's better to follow the educational model. Here the purpose of praise is to accurately recognize accomplishments in objective terms so that the child can learn a realistic, and not inflated, estimate of personal capacity. I believe it is far better for parents to talk in terms of

- *competence,* not excellence,
- *operating ability,* not future potentiality,

- *specific mastery,* not abstract attributes,
- *congratulating personal accomplishment,* not claiming the accomplishment as a source of parental pride.

For example, after watching their fourth-grader perform in a school play, the *booster parents* might be tempted to go over the top in what they say: "You were great! You're going to be a famous actor some day! You spoke your lines like a pro! We're really proud of you!" *Educational parents* might give a different response. "You memorized two pages of lines. You spoke them slowly, clearly, and convincingly. You've learned to perform in front of an audience. Good for you!"

One psychologist notes, "Parents of an only child, I have found, tend to 'inflate' their child, because for one thing, they do see her as the single most wonderful creature in the universe ... And so they are constantly pumping the child up with lots of praise, exploding with delight over some accomplishment for which a sincere 'Good for you' would be more fitting."[5] Another writer provides this caution: "Praise should send an only child the message that he is loved and accepted for the person he is, not for the person parents hope he will become ... Merely stroking them doesn't address their real strengths or help them improve their weaknesses. General praise may lead an only child to think that no one is better than he, no one more special, no one more deserving. That's a dangerous precedent to set."[6]

No wonder the child, believing what her adoring parents say, comes to have an exaggerated sense of her own exceptionality and ability and is set up for a fall when she does not measure up to the unrealistically high self-expectations she has formed. A high-school-age only child in counseling described his jarring entry into first grade this way. "Starting school was probably the biggest shock of my life. At home there had been no competition and no comparison. I came first and no one was better than me. Then suddenly, as one of twenty-some kids, I wasn't the most important anymore. Even worse, I was nowhere near as special as I thought I was. What a comedown!"

School is often the first major change of social reference only children encounter outside of the family. It is the first chance they get to be treated as one of many and to reevaluate their social standing, capacity, and accustomed treatment within a community of competing peers. To the degree that the special valuing received at home has encouraged distorted thinking about themselves, they may bring unrealistic expectations to school.

For only children, adjusting to school can sometimes demand significant self-reappraisal.

- There can be a sense of loss: "I'm not so special after all!"
- There can be a sense of betrayal: "I'm not as smart as my parents told me I was!"
- There can be a sense of disappointment: "I'm not measuring up to what is expected of me!"
- There can be a sense of resentment: "Nobody appreciates how good I really am!"
- There can be a sense of futility: "What's the point of trying if the best I do is not as good as a lot of other students?"

Only children who enter school with an inflated self-image may need some help coming to terms of acceptance with the new picture of how moderately capable they really are. Parents might consider saying to the child something like this. "When you start school you will be one among a large group of children, all equally important to the teacher. In your studies, in some subjects you will do better than some students and in some not as well as others. That is to be expected. You do not have to be the best in everything to do okay. Just pay attention, follow rules, and finish all your work, and where you come out in comparison with others will be good enough."

"You can do anything!" "You can do as well as you want!" "You have the ability to be whatever you want to be!" These kinds of parental messages, intended to express confidence and to give encouragement, can set the child up for disappointment in herself when, out in the adult world, she sadly discovers that

- she can't do everything,
- she can't perform as well as she wishes,
- she lacks the ability to be anything she wants.

One legacy of undue praise in only childhood can be a sense of *relative personal failure* as an adult. No matter how hard she has striven, or sometimes even no matter how much she has accomplished, a troubling feeling of inadequacy is often the result when internalized ideals cannot be met. An adult only child confessed in counseling: "I never measured up to what was expected of me, or at least what I expected of myself. It's taken me a long time to accept that doing moderately well is okay. But every time I see my parents they treat me like they always have—like some kind of extremely accomplished person whom they admire. I always come away feeling mixed. It feels good to be so well thought of, and bad to know I'm not really as wonderful and successful as they want to believe." For many an only child, this sense of disappointment persists so long as she believes that she has not lived up to the lofty ambitions of childhood that parental praise encouraged her to hold.

Researchers described how "one of our adult Onlies remembers how this kind of pressure affected her. She says, 'I always had to be at the top. I couldn't stand anyone else near me. If I thought a teacher didn't like me best, I'd pout and not speak to her for days. In my small rural elementary school I was always at the top, but when I went to college the competition was too stiff. I drove myself into a nervous breakdown."[7] Another adult only child put it this way: "I was bright, and, as the only child, I got more praise than you can imagine. The fallout from that was that I never thought I was good enough. I thought the praise was out of proportion to whatever I'd done, way too much, and I struggled with the level of expectation in myself that grew out of this. I felt pressure to perform, to be worthy of all that praise. Even today, there are some leftovers from this."[8]

If one pitfall in childhood is excessive parental praise, another, later, is excessive criticism of the adolescent who, in service of separation, differentiation, and independence, now dares to displease those adults whose approval still matters to him most of all.

ADOLESCENCE: THE TEMPTATION TO CRITICIZE

Adolescence comes hard to the only child because childhood was usually so harmonious and close. Now there is more personal estrangement and conflict with parents as the time for growth away from family toward more social independence has arrived. Usually unprepared for and disappointed by these developmental changes, parents typically become less understanding and more disapproving, and that makes the child's adolescent transformation harder to bear. *Adolescence is particularly unwelcome* is a harsh truth of only-child growth for parents and the teenager who must now push against and pull away from those who still matter to her most.

In the words of one only child in college looking back: "When I was very young it felt like growing up in the constant glow of my parents' approval. I wanted to do my best to please them, and they wanted to do their best to please me. That was why those early years were so happy and felt so full of love. And it worked wonderfully well, until I hit middle school. Then we began to act in ways each other didn't like. To argue more and fight. I complained and rebelled. They criticized and corrected. It was a hard time. Neither of us felt as loved as we did before."

For all adolescents, but particularly for an only child who is so closely connected to parents, adolescence is an *act of courage*. She must *dare* to be more different and more distant and disagree more with parents than before, risking the disapproval and dislike of the most important people in her world. It is to honor the courage that adolescence entails that parents must *not* criticize the only child during this scary time. *They must not cut off praise and approval.* They must continue to find positive ways to affirm and connect with the teenager during this more contentious period of growth.

When more correction is required, it must be given in a nonevaluative way, focusing on decisions made, not on judging the character of the child. The correction mantra is: *"We disagree with the choices that you made, here is why, and in consequence this is what we need to have you do."* Parents must view any infractions as the exception, not the rule, and always treat the problem as a small part of a large person who mostly conducts herself in meritorious ways. Because they now have more incidents of opposition and misbehavior that require correction, they must find positive ways to engage to offset these negatively experienced times, connections that remind everyone of their unbroken love and capacity for enjoyment of one another. And parents must maintain perspective on the process of adolescence by being adequately informed about the schedule of normal growth changes and what to expect. (For a specific description of how four stages of adolescence typically unfold, see my book *The Connected Father.*)

Maintaining perspective means that parents are knowledgeable enough about the normal course of adolescence that they do not take any of these changes personally and so emotionally overreact, making a difficult situation worse. They need to understand that their only child is doing none of these things *to* them, only *for* herself, and that if other parents were in their place, she would still be acting in most of the same ways. They need to understand that adolescent behavior is of a *trial,* not *terminal* nature. They must wait until her mid- to late twenties to see how she "turns out" as an adult—usually much more similar to them than different.

During the child's adolescence, the parents' job is to keep the expression of caring constant, keep communication open, keep affirming the positive, and hold your only child to responsible account. *This is not a time for depriving her of approvals. In a time of change and insecurity your teenager actually needs your acceptance and approval more than ever before.*

In addition, parents should remember the importance of adult approval in the only child's life. It provides a powerful counterbalance to the need for peer group acceptance that can often lead children who grow up with siblings astray. It is largely because of identifying with parents and other significant adults, and striving for adult standing among them, that the only child is more influenced by gaining adult respect than concerned whether peers will approve or disapprove.

SUMMARY

Children with siblings not only share their parents but also share in satisfying their needs; the only child undertakes to please parents alone. What eases the only child's burden is the undivided attention and extreme admiration she receives in return, which causes her to think well of herself, usually in more exceptional than ordinary terms.

During the only child's early years, parents and child please each other, so much so that the family can feel like a mutual appreciation society in which displeasure can be hard to bear. It is at this point that parental love and approval can become confused for the child, and parents must differentiate between the two so their disapproval is in no way interpreted as a loss of love.

This early dedication to pleasing parents can have a formative effect. Many adult only children who are very concerned with pleasing significant others, being well thought of, and maintaining a good social reputation, are easily upset when any disapproval comes their way.

Only children are often overpraised as they grow up by parents smitten by the wonders of their offspring. As a result the children can develop an exaggerated estimate of personal importance, capacity, and potentiality that proves unrealistic when they enter the larger world. For some adult only children, the outcome can be a nagging sense of disappointment or failure when they do not fulfill the promise that parental praise inspired.

The falling away from parental approval in adolescence can be particularly hard on the only child and the parents as more conflict and less communication combine to allow social separation and independence to grow. This is a time when parents must not let disapproval rule the relationship with their teenager. They must find ways to affirm the worth of their son or daughter as adolescence is causing them to grow apart.

14

DEPENDENCE

A Matter of Holding On

Being raised as an only child usually feels very secure. Staunch parental support creates a strong dependence that the child can rely on and trust. This is a powerful birthright that allows him to develop his own individual definition and follow his own personal direction. He is confident that his parents are always there. In addition, the dependability of parents fosters a similar dependability in the child. Even in adolescence, his word is generally good and his commitments can be counted on. He is reliable. On the problematic side, however, it can happen that parents will not reduce their support and lessen dependency as the child grows, or the child will not accept doing without what the parents have always provided. In situations like this, it can be difficult for the child to separate from the parents without feeling homesick when young or frightened when older, and it can be difficult for parents to relinquish support without fearing a loss of standing with the child and of control over the child's life.

As one writer well states, "The ultimate goal in child rearing is to bring up another human being who can live independently of you."[1] In light of this objective, dependence is probably the trickiest of the fifteen family dynamics described in this book for parents of an only child to manage well, because it can cut in two opposing ways. On the one hand, by encouraging a dependence that the child can count on, parents establish a strong base of trust from which the child's later independence can grow. Securely attached, the child feels confident in venturing off on her own. On the other hand, fostering undue dependence with excessive control and support can have the opposite effect, the child insecurely clinging to parents from lack of self-reliance. *You don't teach independence by preventing dependence on parents. Rather, you establish a base of dependence on parents the child can trust, and from there encourage the child to gather independence of you as she grows.*

Dependence is not "nothing but negative." It has much about it to positively value, like dependability. It is from the *dependability* of parents that only children learn to become dependable themselves. As one adult only child comments: "Oldest kids are just more dependable, I think, because they're more like their parents."[2] Parents of an only child can be grateful for this quality when adolescence comes, when, for the most part, they can rely on the teenager's word and trust her.

Most parents of only children are very good at establishing a strong attachment the child can rely on. However, as one writer observed, "Sometimes parents of only children can't let go of their children as easily as parents who have more than one. They don't let their only child do things independently as young as children with brothers and sisters are allowed to do things. Since the parents have no other children to compare with, they might not be aware that the only is ready for a little independence. Since the parents have no younger children, they have no one else to worry about, so they sometimes end up concentrating all their worries and attachments on the one child."[3] One challenge for all parenting, but particularly for parents of an only child, is *letting go* control and granting sufficient freedom of choice so the child can learn responsible independence. Another one is managing the complexity of *support*—how to provide it and to withdraw it as the child grows. The less willing the parents are to let go of control, the longer they continue to fully support the child as she grows, the more dependent that child is likely to become as an adult. Independence is complicated to teach and hard to learn. The only child is usually ambivalent about independence. He wants it so he can act grown up like parents, but he doesn't want to give up all of the comforts of dependency.

INDEPENDENCE

"Achieving independence," according to one writer, "is a gradual thing... No one acquires skills overnight. You can't always go from you doing the thing for her to the child doing the job competently on her own. Life is like learning to read: first the adult reads to the child, then they read together, the child then reads some words by herself with you still there to prompt her, until she gradually takes over and has mastered the skill. So as our child gets older we must explain what we are doing while we are doing it... Children need to learn how to be an adult and do adult things within a controlled setting, and that is usually the home... You can't live life for your child and nor can you prevent him from taking risks and making mistakes... in the end he has to make his own decisions."[4]

In this process of gaining independence, only children have a *special incentive*. Because they identify with their parents, they want to learn to do the grown-up things their parents do. For this reason, there are a lot of independence skills having to do with taking care of oneself, doing for oneself, and making one's own decisions that only children want to learn very young. They take pride in these grown-up skills and carry this desire to act independently into their older and adult years. In fact, parents of an only child sometimes have to throttle back this push for independence when they believe that the child, who wants to be a small adult, is not ready or the risks are too high.

An important part of childrearing is training the child in all kinds of independent decision making, from walking by himself to the bus stop for elementary school to learning to drive a car in high school. In each case, the training requires preparing the child to exercise this independence responsibly—acquiring sufficient knowledge and acting with sufficient care that a new freedom of choice is safely and effectively managed. This process requires parents to decide what part of the child's life they are ready to *risk* letting go, and what training they are *ready* to provide.

Considering the child's life, where do they still want to retain controlling choice and when do they allow the child to be in charge? How will they decide what remains up to the parents and what they are willing to leave to the child? What to eat, when to go to bed, what to wear, what entertainment to watch, where to go on the Internet, what friends to have, what schoolwork to manage, what household help to provide, what hygiene to take care of. The list goes on and on. At some point they are going to turn these decisions over to the child, but *when* requires serious deliberation. There is no developmentally ordained right time, and no two sets of parents will follow the same schedule. At best, *they grant independence at the point the child is able to honor the new freedom responsibly and does not abuse the privilege.*

Before deciding what area of independent decision making to release, parents have to assess the child's existing record of responsibility and level of maturity. Just because their only child has reached driving age, for example, does not mean they are obliged to allow him to drive if they believe, based on evidence at hand, they would be putting an impulsive and distractible mid- to late adolescent behind the wheel of a car. *When in doubt, wait.* And when ready, commit to the training required, following basic instructional steps.

1. Demonstrate and explain how to do.
2. Support and advise while helping how to do.
3. Supervise and correct by monitoring performance.
4. Allow controlled practice within safe and sheltered limits.
5. Turn over responsibility to the child and let independent learning begin.
6. Credit good choices and require that the consequences of bad ones be faced.

Training their only child for significant independence often requires labor-intensive work, and it is always risky. Allow too much independence too early and parents put the child at risk of immature judgment. *Permissiveness provides no protection.* Allow too little independence and parents put the child at risk of costly inexperience in later decision making. *Prohibition provides no preparation.* Because parents of an only child are so conscientious, how much dependence to demand ("Check with us first") and how much independence to grant ("You decide") require constant consideration. This is said because the only child tends to take it seriously and is usually conscientious, too. When she expresses a readiness for more independence, she often is.

Only children learn independence early, partly by being given more choice, but also partly by taking it. An adult only child described learning independence this way: "I gained experience making choices... Of course I knew the responsibility was mine once I chose something, so I chose very carefully. But the opportunity to do so was exciting, it taught me a lot, and it's one of the things I remember gratefully... I was allowed to make my own decisions with confidence. There was no brother or sister to say, 'That's stupid,' or, 'That's dumb'... As a result, I think I developed a good sense of responsibility: by being allowed to be responsible for my own course of action."[5]

LETTING GO

For the only child to learn independence, parents must learn to let go. In the words of one parent: "'It's hard to let go of an only child... Your child is getting older; you don't have another one coming up. To be able to let go is probably the key."[6] Why is letting go so hard for parents of an only child? There is the temptation to protract dependency. "When a couple have a second child they are more than ready to encourage the first to act independently... The older child is pushed out of the nest and must begin to exercise the ability to care for himself which his physical and mental development have provided... There is danger, however, that the parents, with their love focused as it is on the one child will try to keep him from moving ahead."[7] If they manage to begin letting go, however, and can sometimes leave the child alone, one kind of independence does begin to grow.

Part of the only child's independence is rooted in the absence of siblings and the solitary lessons that circumstance can teach. Three adult onlies describe how independence was learned from facing the reality of *aloneness* and learning to depend on themselves.

- "I was taught to be independent... Because I had a lot of time alone at home, I was curious about investigating things. I became a very creative person in order to entertain myself. My strength as an adult comes from that quest to be creative and independent. My grandparents often told me: You only have you."[8]

- "I always grew up thinking that I had to take care of myself, that I had to be there for myself, had to achieve, that there wasn't going to be anyone to take care of me."[9]
- "If you're part of a big family, chances are you always have a place to live, a roof over your head, and you've always got a loan to carry you though. That's something an only child doesn't have . . . In the back of my mind, I know that I belong only to me."[10]

Now consider two definitions of dependency—as *holding on* and as *relying on support*. Start with the first.

DEPENDENCE AS HOLDING ON

Dependence is an act of holding on to what or who feels emotionally important. A loved one, a habit, a beloved object—all can become a source of dependency, something the person is very reluctant to give up or let go of or back off from. For example, a young only child who feels closely bonded with parents, and is used to having them as constant caregivers and favorite friends, can be reluctant to give up this primary companionship, even for a little while.

- "Don't take private time and make me play by myself!"
- "Don't go out and leave someone else to stay with me!"
- "When you go out, you should take me along!"
- "Why should I stay at my friend's overnight when I'd rather be home having fun with you!"

The journey to independence can be scary for the only child, since growing up means giving up dependency. Social separation from parents can create anxiety: "Can I be okay alone?" To teach the capacity to be by himself and apart from parents, which after the first adjustment most only children seem to learn very well, parents must be willing to leave the child *alone,* leave the child *behind,* and to send the child *off,* each time with the loving assurance (if needed) that they will be back together soon.

Fast-forward to the end of adolescence, when, for adult independence to be claimed, parents must stop holding on, must reset the boundaries of personal responsibility, must let the only child stand on his own in four fundamental ways.

- On *emotional* terms, he must be able to say: "I no longer expect my parents to help me through unhappy times. I can manage the downs and upsets, hurts and disappointments in my life without calling on them."
- On *management* terms, he must be able to say: "I no longer expect my parents to solve my problems or rescue me from situations I get into. I can cope with the consequences of my own bad decisions without their help."
- On *social* terms, he must be able to say: "I no longer expect my parents to be my primary *social* companions. I can form significant, satisfying relationships apart from them."
- On *economic* terms, he must be able to say: "I no longer expect my parents to take care of me financially. I can earn and pay my own way."

Parents who cannot let go encourage an older adolescent to keep holding on, enabling dependency sometimes long after the age for independence has arrived. When parents

- can't stand seeing their older child in pain from normal adversity and rush in to assuage her emotional hurt;
- can't stand seeing their older child get in trouble and provide emergency rescue from bad decisions;
- can't stand seeing their older child alone and substitute themselves for social company;
- can't stand seeing their older child in financial need and pay for what she owes or cannot afford—

they allow their own anxiety to undermine their child's honorable struggle with the demands of independence.

At these moments of temptation, parents may want to keep in mind that sometimes *the hardest help to give is no help at all*. Then, in witness to their love for their only child, they can communicate appropriate support: "We believe you have what it takes to work through this challenge and come out the other side better able to fully function on your own." At the time, your struggling child may not fully appreciate this statement of support.

Of course, in this highly technological age, parents can appear to have let go of their only child in a traditional sense, the child living apart and independently of them, yet they still powerfully hold on. By daily Internet and cell phone communication, parents can keep close tabs on his whereabouts and well-being. Thus one only child in his early twenties described "unplugging" from his parents. Electronic access denied.

The dependent quality of holding on can come to characterize many adult only children whose controlling ways often have more to do with maintaining dependency than a desire for power. They want their partner available and attentive, they want their routines uninterrupted, and they want their significant possessions well taken care of.

Dependency can be a complex issue for adult only children. As two researchers note, "Only children want to be in control, to be close, to be very involved—but on their terms, not someone else's . . . Only children have had a close relationship only with those on whom they are dependent, their parents . . . This means that the only child may be confused about whether he is seeking a relationship in which he is dependent, or one in which he is independent. He is often unaware that the best kinds of relationships are those in which dependency switches around, where the people involved alternate roles."[11]

What parents need to teach their only child is that in significant relationships it's not a matter of *either* dependence *or* independence, but creating an aptitude for *both*. This can become particularly clear in adolescence if parents and child can learn to do *the dance of holding on and letting go,* of providing dependence and encouraging independence, of spending time together and time apart, of agreeing to share some choices and to separately make others. In mature relationships, dependence and independence need not be at war; they can be complementary.

Of course, with parents and only child there is a two-way dependency that must be ended in adulthood if independence is to be gained.

Parents need to be able to let go and live free of the need to worry and identify with the child, and the child needs to become free to make another primary attachment and set forth on an autonomous path. Independence doesn't mean that they won't continue to love each other, communicate with each other, and see each other; it's just that their lives will no longer revolve around each other. One only-child writer observes, "Parents of only children do tend to be hurt and disappointed if they're asked to back off. But their children's emotional growth demands it."[12] Sometimes parents, unhappy with adolescent changes, will try to treat their teenager in childlike ways to recreate the old harmonious relationship they love and miss. Remembering old times, proposing old activities to do together again, even giving the kinds of objects the child used to enjoy—all can be used to hold on to things as they used to be between them in her childhood. In most cases this doesn't go over well with the adolescent who resents this parental expression of dependency at an age when she is pushing for more independence.

A common dependence in adult only children is on adult authority, a dependence that began with parents in childhood and in various forms came to characterize their adult lives.

Most people think of only children as being independent, and they are—as far as their relationship with peers. But only children are very dependent on adults. They come into a room filled with adults and children, and only children are more likely to gravitate toward the adults. They're more comfortable around adults, and they need adult attention, which, I suspect, is why they're achievement-orientated. They're trying to please their parents, and later on their teachers, their bosses, their Army sergeants. The only child's great respect for authority reflects the powerful influence of parents. The only child learns, quite early, that these other authority figures are extensions of their parents...Because of their dependence on adults and their need to please, only children carry an enormous sense of responsibility and loyalty that at times can hinder breaking away and leading their own lives without guilt or regret.[13]

Dependence in the form of compliance with established authority seems to be one defining characteristic of most adult only children, particularly in the workplace, where they are inclined to accept directions, follow procedures, go through channels, and not make waves by getting crossways with or challenging their superiors. (They can, however, be highly controlling and demanding with subordinates.) They tend to be rule followers more than rule breakers, *socially obedient* respecters of the powers that be.

A second source of dependency in only children is their reliance parental support.

DEPENDENCY AS RELYING ON SUPPORT

When it comes to giving support, the task for parents of an only child is to *be dependable without enabling dependency* as the child grows, to be there for the child, but to do less for her as she learns to do more for herself. Done precisely, the process requires perfect timing, parents handing off one additional degree of independence as the child responsibly takes it on. Of course, the timing is never perfect because the weaning from parental support is hard to get exactly right. When parents want to let go, the child wants to hold on: "You ask the teacher why I got that grade, not me. I'm too embarrassed!" When parents want to hold on, the child wants to be let go: "I can handle making my own doctor's appointment; you don't have to do it for me!" When to support and when not to support, that is the question.

To figure out a rough progression for weaning their only child from dependency, parents can distinguish between *primary support* (loving commitment) and *secondary support* (caretaking) that they provide. Different types of activity are included in each kind. The rule is:

- Parents should begin by giving both levels of support.
- They should *never* withdraw primary support.
- As the child grows, they must gradually withdraw secondary support.

Primary support includes being a source of:

- Loving: "Accept me."
- Companionship: "Be with me."

- Listening: "Hear me."
- Confiding: "Tell me."
- Faith: "Believe in me."
- Encouragement: "Cheer me on."
- Empathy: "Feel for me."

Secondary support includes being a source of:

- Instruction: "Explain to me."
- Direction: "Advise me."
- Help: "Rescue me."
- Service: "Do for me."
- Control: "Decide for me."
- Protection: "Look out for me."
- Provision: "Pay for me."

After your child is born and throughout the very early childhood years she needs to have full claim on *both* primary and secondary support to feel secure. As she grows through late childhood and then adolescence, your primary support goes on undiminished, and the transfer of secondary support begins. By adulthood secondary support becomes his responsibility. Transferring responsibility in adolescence can be facilitated when parents ask themselves: "What are we doing for our teenager that he could start learning to do for himself?" Then they turn that over to him.

This transfer is not simple when parents don't want to let the child's reliance on them go, or when the young person doesn't want to take that reliance on. Parents may want hold on to a needed role in their older child's life in order to feel securely connected, to feel of use, and sometimes the child either lacks the inclination or confidence to accept more self-support responsibility.

Then, at the age of young adulthood, when she is still hanging on to parents, they finally weary of her dependence and feel ready to let go. "We keep giving her another chance to get on her feet, but our help just keeps her coming back for more. It's like the more we help, the less she's willing to let us go!" So, in extreme frustration, parents suddenly draw the line, cutting the child off from all problem solving and financial support, saying no to requests and meaning it, perhaps for the first time. "You are going to have to figure out how to take care of yourself and do it on your own. We are not helping you anymore!" For the child, trained to dependence into her twenties, this decision can be both frightening and angering. "But what will I do if I can't manage? This isn't fair! Don't you love me any more?" And she feels a terrible sense of betrayal and rejection by her parents, resentful for being abandoned by those who have always stood behind her. At this late stage, weaning her from their support can be experienced as harsh treatment indeed.

What is sad when events come to this pass is that a crisis was not necessary. In her adolescence, the parents should have started weaning the only child, encouraging and insisting that she take on those secondary self-support responsibilities. Now the child feels blamed for not acting sufficiently mature when it was the parents who enabled this dependency to grow. It is particularly sad when disgusted parents withdraw their primary support, or the older only child believes that with loss of caretaking support has come loss of that primary commitment.

Parents aside, however, adult only children I have seen tend *not* to reach out for support. They have grown up going it alone. They are used to being by themselves, deciding for themselves, and taking care of themselves, so the notion of reaching out for social or emotional support outside of parents leaves them feeling vulnerable and exposed. For sure, trying to persuade an adult only child to join a support group to benefit from the collective wisdom of others who share some common experience and concern has often proved difficult in my counseling. In this sense, an only child can be very insular—"independent" in his own eyes, "isolated" in mine. He can be dependent on himself to his cost, determined to go it alone when depending on others could really help. Thus you have the only child's twin vulnerabilities to the issue of dependence. He may rely on parents and the approval of worldly authority too much, but he may also refuse to reach out and rely on support from non-family members enough.

SUMMARY

The only child can be prone to dependence when parents can't *let go of control* of the child's decision making as she grows, and when the child can't resist relying on their *support* at the expense of learning to help herself. In either case, dependence is a matter of holding on.

The goal in rearing the only child, as it is with all children, is to prepare him for independence. In this education, the only child is at a distinct advantage over children with siblings because he so strongly identifies with parents, desiring to imitate their ways and join their adult ranks. Training for independence requires parental judgment about the child's readiness to assume more self-governance responsibility. Weighing when to let go to allow this growth to occur is difficult. Parents have to relinquish some control over the child and put him at risk of mishaps from his choices.

Dependence is holding on to what feels emotionally important— a loved one, a habit, an object, for example. When young, an only child may hold on to parental company, preferring doing that to spending time with peers. At the end of adolescence, the only child must relinquish holding on to parents to start coping on his own.

There is one common legacy of childhood dependency that can carry into adulthood beneficially: The only child may find a loving partner who is as dependable as the loving parents have been. Another legacy is depending on resident authorities in social and employment settings for their approval, much as he did on parental authority growing up.

The degree of dependency is also related to how parents managed various kinds of support as he grew. While primary support that conveys their loving commitment should never be withdrawn, secondary support of a caretaking kind must be diminished so he can learn to support himself. At times in late adolescence or even young adulthood, when parents find it best to reduce secondary support, they must make it clear that their primary support is unwavering.

15

PRESSURE

A Matter of Demand

Only children pressure themselves to accomplish a lot. They are motivated to perform well partly through the desire to gain parental approval and partly to emulate these adult models. High goals cause them to be ambitious. High standards cause them to be exacting. High limits cause them to take on a lot of responsibility. On the problematic side, however, developing a set of performance expectations that are excessively demanding may produce constant stress. Life can become an exhausting struggle to be ambitious, perfect, and responsible *enough*.

In counseling, I have seen two major sources of stressful pressure on the only-child family: parental *inexperience* and parental *expectations*. Each is demanding in its own way.

PARENTAL INEXPERIENCE

"Many only children undoubtedly suffer," according to two researchers,

> because parents are inexperienced... The parents of an only child have no margin for error... The parents are afraid. They worry and tense up and make the never-easy job of caring for a baby harder and harder. Their anxiety and their fatigue are quickly reflected by the baby, and so a vicious cycle starts... If a second comes along with reasonable promptness, they take in their stride matters that made them

run to call the doctor for the first. They know now that children have a way of surviving. They face their problems calmly and with confidence. The resulting peace is good for everyone, including the older child, though there may still be some truth in the idea that first children tend to grow up tense and overactive. Their parents relax too late. For the Only there is no automatic relief from parental anxieties.[1]

Parental inexperience with other children is often manifest in anxious overreaction to their only child during the normal trials of adolescence. They tend to hold their teenager to extremely intolerant account by exaggerating, magnifying, and even catastrophizing minor problems, turning them into major crises. One daughter in counseling puts it this way to her parents to bring them back to reality: "All I did was flunk a class for not turning in a project, and you're treating me like I'm a total failure, like I don't do anything right! You talk about how I've given up on my education, how I'm in danger of dropping out of school and ending up living in the street. Get real! The rest of my grades are fine and I'll bring this one up next marking period. Everybody blows a class in high school sometimes. It happens! If you knew all the kinds of trouble other kids get into in high school, trouble that I don't get into, you might appreciate how good you've got it with me!"

And, in general, the teenager is correct. Only children, even during the more adventurous adolescent passage, tend to be pretty conservative risk takers, more socially obedient than not, and wed to fulfilling parental expectations if they realistically can. So parents need to maintain perspective when mistakes and missteps occur. Perhaps the following anonymous piece of Internet wisdom can help this process along.

A father passing by his son's bedroom was astonished to see the bed was nicely made and everything was picked up. Then he saw an envelope propped up prominently on the center of the bed. It was addressed, "Dad." With the worst premonition, he opened the envelope and read the letter with trembling hands:

Dear Dad,
It is with great regret and sorrow that I'm writing you. I had to elope with my new girlfriend because I wanted to avoid a scene

with mom and you. I've been finding real passion with Joan and she is so nice—even with all her piercings, tattoos, and her tight Motorcycle clothes.

But it's not only the passion dad, she's pregnant and Joan said that we will be very happy. Even though you don't care for her as she is so much older than I, she already owns a trailer in the woods and has a stack of firewood for the whole winter.

She wants to have many more children with me and that's now one of my dreams too. Joan taught me that marijuana doesn't really hurt anyone and we'll be growing it for us and trading it with her friends for all the cocaine and ecstasy we want. In the meantime, we'll pray that science will find a cure for AIDS so Joan can get better; she sure deserves it!!

Don't worry Dad, I'm 15 years old now and I know how to take care of myself. Someday I'm sure we'll be back to visit so you can get to know your grandchildren.

Your son, John

P.S.: Dad, none of the above is true. I'm over at the neighbor's house. I just wanted to remind you that there are worse things in life than my report card that's in my desk center drawer. I love you! Call when it is safe for me to come home.[2]

Usually, parents of an only child must be one-trial learners because they have not had a child before. Trial and error is how parents must proceed. Fear of error is inherent in their parenting; that anxiety is part of the emotional fabric of the family as the child grows up. What parents must remember is that when they imagine worst-case scenarios that affect their attitude and determine their speech, they will stress their only child with their fears. Maintaining perspective when troubles inevitably arise is one of the hardest and most important jobs that come with parenting an only child. Fear only causes them to foresee troubles ahead.

Frequently, one of my jobs in counseling with an only child family is helping everyone look at the big picture of what is going on after some teenage misadventure. I do this not to deny the problem but to help restore the positive perspective that parents have lost to extreme worry and that the child has lost from listening to parental fears. So with parents who are distraught that their only child has had a serious lapse of judgment from substance use at a high school party, I try to help them see that "all is not lost," that their daughter is exercising very good judgment in other areas of her life. For example, during her first two years of driving there have been no moving violations or accidents. She has held a part-time job for over a year, saving most of her money. She takes care of homework and is an honor student. She does her chores at home without being asked, and keeps her curfew. "Deal with the problem," I encourage them, "but also recognize that it is the exception to what is mostly going very well."

Keeping perspective means that parents see their child in context, as a person who is infinitely larger than the sum of his problems. This global vision allows them to effectively approach whatever is going wrong with a balanced estimate that also credits all that is going right. Drawing upon these strengths helps the child recover from the difficulty of the moment. A greater source of stressful pressure on only-child families than parental inexperience and loss of perspective, however, is parental expectations.

PARENTAL EXPECTATIONS

Parents and an only child try very hard to do right by each other, paying a heavy emotional price when either feels they have let down or done the other wrong. It's not so much that parents and child demand a lot from each other, although they usually do, as that they demand so much from themselves. *This is a striving family.* Parents put a lot of performance pressure on themselves, and when they do, they put a lot of pressure on the only child, who wants to live up to their example and please them too, thus putting a lot of pressure on himself. The terms "laid-back" and "relaxed" usually do *not* describe parents and their only child.

The only-child family is one in which *performance expectations* in the form of *goals* and *standards* and *limits* are highly demanding. In the words of one psychologist: "In my practice, I have met wonderful, caring, terribly eager and earnest parents who are determined to do right by their only child . . . They are able and eager to expend time and sometimes considerable resources in giving their one child what they intend to be a perfect start in life . . . They plan to raise a child they can view with pride as well as love—with satisfaction in their own 'job well done.' . . . Trouble looms, however, when a parent, with perhaps the best intentions, consistently pressures a child to become what he cannot be or does not want to be, to become a 'superchild' who shines in all areas."[3]

Here are what a few sources have to say about the pressure of growing up only.

- "My parents have always expected me to be a 'good' kid, but sometimes I just want to break out. They expect me to be perfect. You know, be a great student, do my chores, choose the right friends. It's a lot of pressure. If I had a brother or sister, I don't think they would notice me so much."[4]
- "Some only children often become achievers because they are expected to be all things to two people . . . Parents have high expectations whether they have one child or three, but the screws seem to turn a little tighter on one child . . . 'I felt enormous pressure. Because I was an only child, I had to be everything.'"[5]
- "If parental focus becomes burdensome, the child is pressured— perhaps to return an undue amount of affection, perhaps to achieve honors beyond his ability or desire."[6]
- "For all offspring there is a greater or lesser feeling of tension between what they know or believe their parents want for them and what they want for themselves. This is a natural state of affairs to which the only-child family is no exception. Where it *is* different lies in the fact that parents have only one hope of their ambitions being realised . . . The single child has to carry . . . all such expectations from parents . . . Most [interviewees] felt the pressures as a burden . . . 'Never enough' is the resonant phrase. However hard they tried, only children rarely felt they had achieved as much as was expected of them. And what's the result of all this? Only children tend to be very hard upon themselves. Other's high expectations of them are nothing to what they expect of themselves. The hardest taskmaster for the only child is himself."[7]
- "Without siblings to absorb some of the criticism and to offer support and another view of reality, the only child can begin to feel that the only way to survive is to do whatever is necessary to

get the approval of parents who hold the symbolic power of life and death. It becomes a way of life, even when an only child is not a child anymore."[8]

THE PRESSURE TO PERFORM

Pressures on an only child from striving to perform up to parental expectations are soon internalized into self-expectations by the child, governing beliefs that operate like "inner parents" who must be loyally obeyed, who exert continuing influence as he grows. In the absence of his actual parents, these inner representations encourage him to behave as he was taught. Meet those expectations, and approval from the success causes him to feel happy. Don't meet those expectations, and disappointment from failure causes him to feel unhappy. He is under constant pressure to measure up.

If he had siblings he would understand that every child is at best an intermittent and not a flawless performer who meets some parental expectations some of the time, and other expectations not at all. He would understand that when parental expectations are unmet, parents live with this variation and inconsistency, while children adjust to whatever parental disappointment or disapproval the unmet expectation may temporarily create. When he sees older and younger siblings upsetting parents and then life going on, getting in trouble becomes unwelcome but okay.

Because he is the only child, however, he is not given the freedom to be an intermittent performer and to accept parental disappointment or disapproval as normal when their expectations are unmet. In the extreme, he believes in striving to meet *all* their expectations, since his parents believe that he will incorporate the potentialities of all children because they have only one. He tries to be a flawless performer, to avoid letting parental expectations down—to the unhappiness of all. In addition, he has usually been encouraged to be a "can-do thinker," having been told he can do anything with himself and his life that he puts his mind and effort to. So heed this advice to parents: *"Recognize that all your expectations, fantasies, hopes, and dreams are invested in one child. And perceive how easily that can create pressures for your child and for you."*[9]

Of course, if parents expected nothing of the child, leaving him to form his own expectations as he grew, there would be no pressure; but this is a freedom parents cannot responsibly provide. Part of their job when he is young is to set three kinds of performance expectations based on what they want him to learn to do, and how well they want him to do it, and on the multiplicity of demands they think he is capable of handling. To this end they set:

- *Goals* that have to do with the *degree of ambition:* how high to achieve.
- *Standards* that have to do with the *degree of excellence:* how well to get things done.
- *Limits* that have to do with the *degree of responsibility:* how much to undertake at one time.

All three kinds of performance expectations regulate the amount and pressure of demand under which the only child labors. As psychologist Susan Newman points out,

> In their enthusiasm parents often don't realize how much pressure they exert on their children. Watch for danger signals the pressure is too great, that the extra push you think is helping your child is counterproductive. In the younger child, stress shows early. You can tell you are being too demanding when your child begins to turn to your spouse or partner on a regular basis for entertainment, consolation, or affection... She will march to the parent who accepts her skills at her level. Overemphasis on excellence is also easy to spot in the school-age child. A drop in the quality of schoolwork, extreme sensitivity to mild or constructive criticism... are indicative of an overstressed child... Because only children expend great amounts of effort to satisfy their parents, it may be wise to rethink your only's involvement and to listen to what he may be "telling" you. Onlies can be very hard on themselves, so when the pressure seems too much, consider allowing your child to drop an activity, pull back, and ease up... *There is a tendency on the part of the parents to take responsibility for how the child turns out instead of accepting that's how the child is.*[10]

Newman makes a fundamental point that parents of an only child should keep in mind: *Expectations of acceptance* are more important than *expectations of attainment.*

Expectations of acceptance fill the child with an affirming sense of sufficiency:

- "I will do what I can."
- "I want what I have."
- "I should be as I am."

Expectations of attainment fill the child with a motivating sense of dissatisfaction:

- "I will try harder."
- "I want to achieve more."
- "I should make myself do better."

Both sets of expectations are beneficial, but unless those of acceptance come first, the child is set up for stress by developing a *performance identity,* believing:

- "What I am worth is how well I can do."
- "I must do well to be acceptable."
- "If I don't do well, I am not acceptable."

Believing this, the only child is set on the painful path of having to continually prove his worth today, no matter how much he accomplished yesterday. Ceaseless performance pressure will be an abiding part of daily life.

Parents have three responsibilities in managing performance expectations for their only child.

First, starting out when the child is young, parents must set these expectations for her to help encourage healthy growth. To this end they set goals for the child to attain (objectives to accomplish), standards to live up to (level of effort to be made), and limits for encompassing how much the child should do (scope of responsibility). They do this by evaluating the child's ability and interests and by combining this assessment with competencies they believe should be acquired.

Second, somewhere toward the end of high school, parents must begin the emancipation of expectations. They need to explain how it is time for the adolescent to take responsibility for modifying *parental* expectations by making them *personal*, creating a set of goals, standards, and limits that, in her best judgment, fit the individual she has become. These will depart from old parental expectations to some degree, and that is how it should be.

Parents can make clear how they will respect and value whatever performance expectations the teenager decides to follow. If they choose, they can do so by using a modification of the famous "Gestalt Prayer" created by psychologist Fritz Perls. They can say it and mean it: *"From here on, we will do our thing and you will do your thing. We are not in this world to live up to your expectations and you are not in this world to live up to ours. If we happen to meet each others' expectations, that is wonderful. If we don't, it can't be helped. In either case, we will gratefully accept and love you for the person you are, and we hope you will do the same with us."* With these words, or something like them, parents bless the individuality and affirm the independence of both themselves and their only child.

Third, with the emancipation of the older adolescent from parental expectations and the assumption of responsibility for installing her own, the teenager still needs some instruction from parents about how to manage expectations now. Parents need to teach the only child about the relationship between *expectations she elects to set and the amount of work that meeting them will demand.* Continually striving to reach unattainable performance expectations is expensive, because the psychological cost of excessive demands is stress.

Consider the only child in high school who wants to lead her chosen extracurricular activities, excel in all her classes, and satisfy all personal calls that friends make upon her. Come spring semester, her parents find themselves living with someone who is not the relaxed, cheerful, and happy person they knew. She seems tense, tired, and troubled. Although much admired for the work she does and how well she does it, the young woman is operating under more self-imposed pressure than she can comfortably sustain.

In this situation parents may decide to caution their only child about the consequences of her choices. They could say something like this:

> We support your doing well for yourself, but we want you to connect the choices you make with the costs you may pay. How you set your goals, standards, and limits determines how much demand you place on your life. *How high* should you strive? That is the *goal* question. *How well* should you do everything? That is the *standards* question. *How much* responsibility should you undertake at one time? That is the *limits* question. If your answer to the goals question is that you want to *be the best,* if your answer to the standards question is that you must *do everything perfectly,* if the answer to the limits question is that you must *satisfy everyone's needs,* you are going to lead a very high-demand life. And we don't mean just in high school, because how you learn to act now sets the pattern of performance you will follow later on your own. What we wish for you is to be able to define a very simple word in terms that keep you productive, but also happy day to day. That word is *enough.*

- What is enough ambition?
- What is enough perfection?
- What is enough responsibility?

> Because you are an only child, you will always be demanding of yourself, so you must learn to weigh the accomplishment you want against the pressure that demand creates.

Only children who cannot make up their minds about what is *enough* performance set themselves up for ongoing discontent and stress. Those adult only children who cannot emancipate themselves from the performance expectations initially set by well-meaning but demanding parents tend to lead very driven lives.

From what I have observed in adult only children, this sense of being driven can sometimes create a vulnerability to abuse of alcohol or other drugs to chemically unwind, relax, or to escape the unrelenting demands that unmodified parental expectations have shaped. *Better to moderate unrealistic expectations than to self-medicate the resulting stress.*

You must help your older adolescent reset performance expectations because they bear so heavily on the healthy and happy future of your only child.

SUMMARY

Parents and a single child constitute high-pressure families partly because of parental inexperience, but mostly because of parental expectations. From inexperience, parents of an only child tend to magnify and overreact to small problems that parents with multiple children would downplay or even ignore. It is through anxious overreaction, however, that parents can end up stressing themselves and their only child, turning a minor concern into a major crisis. For this reason, these parents need to learn how to maintain perspective; it is an essential skill.

High performance expectations, in the form of goals, standards, and limits that parents set, and that the only child incorporates, create the greatest pressure. Striving to live up to these expectations, and seeking to be a person free from faults, seem to be major objectives of the only child who doesn't want to let parents down. Parents can help allay these pressures. In addition to setting realistic and modest expectations that comfortably fit the child, they can separate expectations of acceptance from expectations of attainment, always putting acceptance first so the child doesn't grow up believing that self-worth depends upon performance.

Since performance expectations create demands, moderating the expectations can prevent overdemand that can lead to stress. Key to managing moderation is helping the child determine what constitutes enough ambition, enough excellence, and enough responsibility, because all three will remain salient issues in adult life. Common adult outcomes for an only child having high self-expectations: She is ambitious to achieve, drawn to perfection, and conscientious about her responsibilities.

16

ANXIETY

A Matter of Loss

Only children are given a lot. Unrivaled by siblings, they are closely connected to parents in two powerful ways. First, because they feel so well attached to parents, a sense of security grows. And second, because they strive to be like their parents, a similarity develops that creates a strong common bond. In many aspects of life, from interests to aspirations to values, parents and child are on the same page. On the problematic side, however, are two powerful sources of anxiety that develop as the child grows. They can limit her development, particularly in adolescence, when more social separation and personal differentiation must be done to attain independence.

I believe *growing up is giving up,* because all growth entails loss—of what one used to have and of how one used to be. For the only child, significant anxiety can be experienced at two particularly difficult giving-up points.

- Because attachment is so close, growing *separation from parents* can be scary.
- Because similarity is so pronounced, growing *differentiation from parents* can be scary.

Separation causes parents anxiety because more distance creates a loss of control, whereas there is more anxiety in the child from feeling less securely tethered to them. Differentiation causes parents anxiety more from unfamiliarity with the person the child is becoming, whereas there is more anxiety in the child from fearing parental disapproval of her change. Threat of both losses combine in the only child's adolescence when she can fear that by becoming too separated and too different from them, she may strain or even break their traditionally harmonious connection to one another.

For the child,

- *separation anxiety* is caused by the fear of disconnection with parents, and
- *differentiation anxiety* is caused by the fear of disapproval from parents.

In the worst case, which everyone hopes does not happen, parents make statements when impatient that can inflame both anxieties in the young child. They can inflame separation anxiety by saying something like: "If you don't come with me right now, I'm going to leave you behind!" They can inflame differentiation anxiety behavior by saying something like: "If you don't stop acting that way, I'm going to disown you!"

From what I have seen in counseling, these two anxieties tend to shape common vulnerabilities in marriage for an adult only child. *Loss of closeness when emotional or physical distance of a partner is experienced, and loss of acceptance when criticism or disapproval by that partner are expressed, can be sources of significant anxiety. In each case, they are often amplified by earlier childhood and adolescent fears.*

SEPARATION ANXIETY

"Very often," one writer observes, "only children find it hard to do anything without their parents. All their lives they have been included in most of their parents' activities. Breaking away may be more difficult than for a child from a large family."[1]

The amount of anxiety over separation is proportional to the time spent apart from parents. Parents who will not put the only child down, leave the child alone, allow the child some discomfort, or entrust the child's care to someone else, may make necessary separations later on a larger challenge. Being left with a sitter, going to daycare, leaving home for elementary school, or sleeping overnight at a friend's can all create wrenching separations for an only child unaccustomed to being away from parental care. On these occasions, most of the homesickness is anxiety over questions that are worrying the only child:

- "Will they miss me when I'm gone?"
- "Will they be there when I return?"
- "Will they be okay without me?"
- "Will I be okay without them?"
- "Suppose I need to talk with them when I'm away?"
- "Suppose I get in trouble and they're not around?"
- "Suppose there's no one there to care for me as well as I'm cared for at home?"

One antidote for homesickness (when the emotional strain of missing home can cause physical complaints like aches, nausea, and sleeplessness) is encouraging the young only child to ask questions in advance so they can be discussed and his worst fears allayed. Also by declaring that their first significant separation from the child will take *them* some getting used to, parents can give the child permission both to expect and accept some adjustment himself. "We'll miss you and you'll probably miss us. And that's okay because we haven't done this before." Two researchers propose that

Several psychological influences may combine to cause homesickness. The child, off in new surroundings, is deprived of support of his normal routine. If the new situation is both strange and difficult, the child may "run away" in his thoughts and do nothing but think of that safe, happy place, home. The child may fear that his parents have sent him away because they do not love him, that he has, in effect, been abandoned... Time to get used to the new surroundings is the great cure... If his homesickness is due to a tendency to withdraw from difficult situations, permitting him to

withdraw confirms him in a bad habit. The girl who is allowed to
abandon school because she is homesick may very well be the one
who "runs home to mother" instead of trying hard to make her
marriage work. We'd suggest, rather, that the parents be firm in stating that the child must remain . . . If either parent was ever homesick, the child can be helped by being told the circumstances of
onset and recovery. Just knowing that one's parents know how one
feels is a comfort.[2]

An adult only child feels this variation of homesickness: "I feel really unsettled and anxious when my retired parents go on foreign
travel. Away on these trips, they are not in place, they are hard to
reach, I am left alone, and I don't sleep well until they return." Because the only child grows up so intertwined with parents, she can feel
discomfort with separation from them even at this older age.

Facing the normal anxiety in life that comes from separation from
home and entering a new and untried situation is what the only child
must learn how to do. Departure from parental care does not signify
abandonment; rather it marks a significant step in the child's growing
up. Encouraging the child to take that step is part of the parents' job.

Sometimes, parents can inadvertently make a difficult separation
worse. An only child who experiences significant separation anxiety
starting school, for example, often has parents who fear letting go.
Typically, these are well-meaning parents who offer reassurance to the
child and themselves in ways that only makes both sets of fears much
worse.

"That's not true," objects a parent in counseling, proceeding to
describe how it is only the only child who is unwilling to let go.

We've supported our child in every way we can. We've got
this elaborate good-bye ritual we go through every day before
school—answering the same questions over and over again.
We've gotten special permission from the counselor to let our
child call us at lunch. We take our child to the classroom
door each day to prevent having to walk down the hall alone.
We've even given our child a "magic" coin to hold to stop the
fear—a lucky piece I used to carry. We've taken every measure

we can think of to make our child feel secure at school, but the anxiety hasn't gotten any better. What else can we do?

"Stop scaring the child with all the safety precautions you are taking," I suggest. Such reassurances and protections only convince the child of how well founded his anxieties are. When parents act like there is something to be afraid of, the child learns to be afraid. When they normalize the separation, accept the fear but treat the necessary adjustment with trust and confidence, then that is what the child will finally learn to do.

To make separation anxiety worse, parents can

- be unduly reassuring,
- take unusual measures to protect the child,
- arouse the child's worries with their own,
- become impatient, critical, or angry at the child for feeling afraid.

There is no sin in feeling afraid, particularly of new experiences. All change can create anxiety as one departs the familiar and enters the unknown. For many children, but particularly for only children, separation from parents can feel threatening, leading to a perceived loss of control, closeness, and comfort. When it does, parents need to honor the fear and recognize the strength it takes to overcome being afraid—the courage the child needs to brave his way through a challenging change.

What parents can explain to the anxious child is something like this:

We know you feel scared. At various times in life everyone, including us, feels scared. There is nothing wrong with feeling afraid. Some fear warns us of danger; it says, "Watch out!" Other fear, like being apart from us at school, says, "I've never done this before," or "I'm not used to this yet." Remember that fear is often a liar. It warns that you can't do what you really can. You don't have to do the frightening thing, but you do need to test it out, to *try* it. That way you can see if fear was really telling you the truth or not. What increases fear is running from it. What reduces fear is facing it and seeing what the actual experience is like. When you find it's not as bad as you thought, you will feel more confident in yourself. That's your reward for acting brave.

This fear of separating from home not only occurs at the beginning of elementary school but at the end of high school, as well. Come graduation, it is easy for parents to become worried about their child's readiness to depart their care for more independence. In their only child's late adolescence, it is important that they manage this anxiety without undercutting the only child's courage and resolve to leave. What can help parents at this separation point is to remember that almost no late adolescent child departs from home fully equipped with all the knowledge, skills, and responsibilities required for increased self-support. Whether starting to share an apartment and hold a full-time job, or starting to live in a dorm and go to college, there will be a host of unfamiliar demands and problems for which the only child will be unprepared. Perhaps 60 percent of the preparation needed for independence is about as much as most parents can provide. That done, they must turn their child over to the Big R, Reality, and the School of Hard Knocks, in which he or she must learn the rest. Therefore, if parents insist on delaying the only child's departure until he or she is "all ready," they will never let him go. *Some degree of unreadiness for independence is not a problem for the late adolescent. It is a fact of life.*

What can overcome the child's reluctance to go is irritation with the parents. That motivates the only child take the plunge into more independence. In the words of one such client, "The greatest incentive I have for leaving home is the aggravation of still living there, of having to put up with parents who really get on my nerves!" That's one function of adolescence. Over time, it creates enough incompatibility and conflict to wear down the dependence between parents and child until they are willing to let each other go.

Fine tuning—trying to cram last-minute lessons for living independently into the only child's senior year of high school—usually just provokes conflict and reinforces what the child already fears: "I don't yet know enough to make the next step on my own." As for parents' directly expressing worry to the late adolescent about harmful possibilities that might occur, these are usually received by the older teenager as a vote of no confidence when his own self-confidence is already feeling pretty low. Because their child has enough worries of his own, parents do better not to burden him with any more, but to keep them between themselves. What the late adolescent needs is a strong statement of faith by parents that he has what it takes to learn from new experiences the necessary skills for independent living.

What makes the child's leaving hard for parents is the new emptiness at home. Filling up their lives in other ways and staying in touch with the child who still wants to stay in touch with them makes the separation bearable. Then the only child takes on a life partner, and that event usually finalizes the social separation between them.

THE LIFE PARTNER

When the adult only child commits to an adult relationship, anxiety-provoking issues can be raised about integrating two loves—for parents and for partner. Growing up in an only-child family, the young person experienced *undivided love*. Having no other children, the parents entirely dedicated their love to the single child, who was totally devoted in return. In consequence of this exclusive love, the attachment between parents and child became very secure, and a strong sense of loyalty—an allegiance to each other's well-being—developed. On both sides of the relationship, each wants to do right by the other and treats the welfare of each other as a high priority concern.

When the only child enters young adulthood, leaving home and claiming independent self-support, her sense of loyalty to parents is often increased by obligation, which is expressed in a variety of ways.

- "I owe my parents a lot for all they've done for me."
- "I need to remain an active part of their lives after I leave."
- "I should be there for them if they need me."
- "I want to let my parents know how much they matter to me."
- "I want to keep them first in my concerns, as they keep me in theirs."

At best, assuming the trials of adolescent conflict have done no lasting damage, the relationship between parents and adult only child is a reward they all enjoy: "We love being together, we are dearest friends." It is when the adult only child develops a serious romantic attachment, however, that undivided love can feel like it must become divided. Then, old loyalty to parents becomes conflicted. For the first time, the child's love becomes significantly attached to someone outside of the family.

Now the challenge is how to separate love for parents from love for the romantic partner, without feeling one is betraying or lessening the love for parents. This is when anxiety based on loyalty can arise for the only child: "How can I love someone else and not have my parents feel I love them any less?"

At this juncture, parents can be very helpful or very harmful, depending on how they choose to respond.

They can be harmful if they act as if:

- They feel *demoted* in importance at having now become only a secondary concern for the child;
- They feel *rejected* in favor of someone who now receives the love that once was theirs;
- They feel *abandoned* and have much less contact with their child;
- They feel *jealous* of a rival who has stolen their place in the child's affections.

Acting on any of these feelings usually results in expressions of disapproval, criticism, or opposition, and they in turn cause the adult only child, torn between two loyalties that seem irreconcilable, to feel anxiety and guilt.

- "Why am I made to feel I have to choose between love for my parents and love for my intended?"
- "Must I divorce my parents to marry the person I love?"
- "It's not the person I'm in love with who my parents don't like, it's my being in love with anyone at all."
- "No one I marry will ever be good enough for my parents because they don't want to share me with anyone else."

They can be helpful by assisting in the reconciliation process that is troubling their child by offering some simple explanations.

- "Loving someone else doesn't decrease your love for us, it only increases the love you have to give."
- "Parental love and partner love do not compete because they are different kinds of love, the first based on family attachment, the second on chosen commitment."
- "Time with your loved one does not take your love away from us because we always hold you in our hearts, whether together or apart, and we know you do the same with us."
- "Putting your romance or marriage first does not mean you love us any less; it means you must honor and invest in this new relationship if you want it to develop."
- "Seeing you love someone else is not a source of loss for us, but of joy to see you happy in a love of your own."

When an only child gets married, a second level of loyalty conflicts can ensue: conflicts of sharing. As families become extended through marriage, commitments become more complex. The only child must now juggle membership in *three* families instead of one.

1. There is the child's original family.
2. There is the family begun with the partner.
3. And there is the partner's family.

Needs of all three families now vie for the only child's attention, creating separate loyalties that can feel conflicting and confusing. When parents insist that loyalty to them comes first ("Of course, we expect you both to celebrate the entire holiday with us"), the only child cannot help but feel torn apart. What about family time with the partner? What about family time with in-laws? "How can I have separate times with my spouse, and with my spouse's family, and not feel guilty about not being with my parents?" The answer is: *Parents have to respect that their married only child has the two other families, so that conflicted loyalties do not become a source of anxiety and guilt.*

To help free their only child from this anxiety, parents can bless her membership in the separate families that have been created.

- "We are happy that now you have more family in your life than before."
- "Just as we welcome your partner into our family with love, we want you to enjoy being welcomed into your partner's family with love."
- "Because you have three families to live in now, and not just one, we expect that you will want to take more time separate from ours to build and enjoy the other two."

Parents of an only child end up having to learn to do something that is a problem often ascribed to their only child. *They have to treat more separation as growth, not abandonment or rejection. They have to learn to gladly share.* They also have to willingly accept the only child's need to differentiate himself from the child he used to be, from the way his parents are, whom he once longed to imitate, and from how they might wish that he turn out to be. And this differentiation can include choosing an adult partner who may be very different from the parents, whom they must learn to accept and welcome with love if they wish to remain closely connected with their beloved child.

DIFFERENTIATION ANXIETY

In a family with multiple children, inevitable human differences between siblings tend to increase parents' tolerance for diversity and can reduce their expectation of similarity, not only among the children, but between each child and themselves. The more children parents have, the more accepting they usually become of individual variation.

In an only-child family, however, those parental tolerance limits tend to be more narrowly defined, because the boy or girl, particularly during the first seven or eight years of life, finds becoming the same as parents a positively natural way to grow. *Similarity to parents is both rewarding* ("I like being like my parents") *and rewarded* ("And my parents like it when I act like them"). Having so much in common is one of the factors that cause parents and only child to feel so close. Dissimilarity can create distance from parents, and the only child can be scared of that. At the extreme is the child who claims so much in common with the parents that he never joins a cultural tribe of peers and never gains the opportunity for differentiation that membership provides.

Differentiation is the adolescent process of redefinition through experimenting with becoming different from how one was as a child, from how parents are, from how parents want the young person to be. It is a process of trying on and putting off a host of different images, aspirations, experiences, and relationships to discover what seems to fit and what does not so that by the end of adolescence the new adult can claim an authentically fitting independent identity: "At last I am my own person!" For parents this process of redefinition can be like watching their perfect child become an imperfect teenager, and they can regret the loss and mourn it: "Whatever happened to the wonderful way she used to be?" *Differentiation anxiety in the child stems from fear of this disappointed and critical response.*

Sometimes the only-child adolescent conforms to parents at the expense of differentiation because she doesn't want to risk courting their disapproval and threatening her good standing in their eyes. The adult result is like what I have seen in counseling over the years—*a grown only child who is extremely well individuated (with a strongly defined personality), but not very well differentiated from what the parents are or from how they want her to be (lacking a satisfying sense of independent identity),* These adult only children usually have some delayed differentiation to do. In the words of one such client: "There were a lot of doors for growth I never opened as a teenager for fear my parents would disapprove." One counselor who was interviewed echoes this tendency of the only child to seek similarity with parents. "'The only child tends to pick up many of the characteristics of the parent to a greater extent than other children.'" The interviewer then added: "And I have often heard that even in the critical, rebellion-prone teen years only children tend to remain fairly close to the basic values of their parents."[3]

How much obliged to stay similar to parents and how much to become different is a developmental question built into adolescence. All children must resolve the issue, but it is particularly anxiety provoking for the only child. Testimony to this hardship comes from two adult only-child subjects.

- "Teenage rebellion? What's that? Only children can't have it in an overt way. You can't really, can you? It's too much of a responsibility. There is only you and it would be too hard on your parents—so you find other ways."[4]
- "In a way it's always been like that—trying to find the adolescence I didn't have."[5]

The researchers further explain, "The desire to conform that only children feel is stronger than the desire to rebel for many of them at the usual teenage rebellion stage. The need to make up for this later in life may be more pronounced with them because they have been more good than other children, from an earlier age."[6] If similarity to how parents are and what they want is the royal road to their approval, differentiation risks leading to the opposite outcome, a risk many adolescent only children are reluctant to take.

For parents of an adolescent only child, this raises one of their most delicate and difficult challenges: to adequately create a sense of fitting in and family belonging for the child while giving sufficient permission for differentiation so he can claim social and psychological independence. For the first and only child, adolescent differentiation can be very hard to achieve.

Testimony to the difficulty of adolescent differentiation is seen in the only child who has delayed trying it until the end of high school, when, in a burst of desperation to become his own person, he defines himself in opposition to everything his parents hold dear. Then a very rough period of transformation can ensue as he engages in self-defeating, even self-destructive behaviors—significant substance use, sexual acting out, failing grades, disregarding home rules meant for his protection—all to show he is not the child he was or the one they want him to be. What parents see is his defiance. What they don't see is the guilt and fear that follow from his breaking the ties that bind. At times like this, family counseling can help. Even in cases like this, after more differentiation has been claimed, the child ends up far more like parents than different. He "falls away" at the time, all right, but in the end it turns out he doesn't fall very far from the family tree.

Birth-order literature explains why firstborn children are reluctant to differentiate: "In comparison to the firstborn's identification with and modeling of parental figures, laterborn children are the beneficiaries of the trial-and-error learning that parents have accrued. Subjected to less parental anxiety and inexperience, and so allowed more freedom to take risks and to try new ways, *laterborn children emerge as more psychologically differentiated* . . . where firstborn children have no consistently present model except that of their parents to emulate."[7]

Another birth-order researcher states: "Everything that is known about siblings indicates that they go out of their way to be different" from each other.[8] Laterborns tend to develop an identity more independent of parents, and be more rebellious, than is likely to be true for the only or first child. What the same researcher calls "radicalism" is the development of extreme differentiation from established beliefs of parents and often of society. "Firstborns tend to respect the status quo, but the second of two children is distinctly radical. As sibship size increases, lastborns continue to be the most radical family members."[9] It is through similarity to parents that the only child protects what the writer calls the "parental investment"—securing all the benefits that parents have to confer.

Desire to maintain this investment, and fear of losing it, make the process of adolescent differentiation particularly anxiety producing. For the only child, engaging with this process is an act of courage because it feels so scary

- to rebel against what one was as a child,
- to no longer fit in and conform to family,
- to become more resistant to parental authority,
- to experiment with self-definitions that may provoke parental disapproval,
- to socially separate from parents in search of independent friendships,
- and to fight for more social freedom than parents may want to give, creating unwelcome conflict in the process.

Diversity of development in any child partly depends on what the parents encourage, tolerate, and allow, but for an only child the need to go along with the parental agenda, down their path, following their directions and opinions and restrictions, is particularly strong. Similarity is rewarded because imitation in this case is not only the sincerest form of flattery, it proves to be the most successful. When an only child acts grown-up, conforms to belong, copies her elders, and behaves the way they like, they reward her with approval and inclusion.

For differentiation to occur in adolescence the young person must *pull away from parents* for more independence and room to grow and must *push against parents* to assert his individuality to claim his own distinct identity. "Only children usually pay close attention to their parents' goals for them. That's acceptable unless and until a child begins to feel so much pressure to conform to his parents' will that he loses individuality in the process."[10] Sometimes an only child will combine conformity with rebellion to get the job of differentiation done. For example, the sixteen-year-old still remains strongly committed to having an active religious life like her parents, but she chooses to change the faith she believes in and the church she attends.

For differentiation to take place, experimentation and contrast must occur, and this can be resisted by the grown only child's holding back as much as by the parents' holding on. "My parents didn't cling to me and didn't encourage me to be dependent on them or to look at them as my only source of nourishment. Yet, I had a terrible time breaking away from home. Why? Mostly it was because I enjoyed a good life there—not in a material way, although I got whatever goodies were available, but from the standpoint of being accepted, listened to, treated with respect, made to feel important."[11] Conformity is comfortable.

One adult only child who threaded the needle of differentiation successfully—claiming her independent identity and having parents who blessed the individual she became—described it this way.

> I think one feels obliged to please these parents; you're all they have. On the other hand, you feel you have to please yourself because you're a human being and you're all that you have. I think that's the conflict of being an only child. There was certainly a period in

which I felt a strong pull to be what my parents wanted me to be. Although that was never exactly defined, I had an idea of what that was. On the other hand, I had just as strong a pull to be what I wanted, although I didn't know what that was either. I just knew it had to be different. Then it turned out, because my parents were good people with good values, what they wanted from me was what I wanted from me. A lot of my own peace comes from the fact that I was all my parents had and I pleased them—and I pleased myself. If I had done one and not the other, I think I would have been in torment.[12]

Another only child reflects how it feels when adequate differentiation is *not* accomplished: "I fantasize now and then about what life would be like without my parents. Aside from the immediate feeling of loss, my first instinct is that I'd finally be able to be myself."[13]

For the adult only child, becoming adequately differentiated during adolescence means having braved anxiety at what might happen if parents either did not understand or disapproved of the search for self that was under way. Inadequate differentiation in adolescence can lead to an adult only child who in counseling expresses a nagging sense of lost possibility, of missing out on a freer, different path of growth that might have led to a more authentic and satisfying sense of personal identity.

SUMMARY

Two progressive losses during growing up that create anxiety for all children can be particularly acute for only children because attachment and similarity to parents are so strong. The first kind of loss is caused by separation, the second by differentiation. Separation anxiety arises in response to the threat of disconnection to parents. Differentiation anxiety arises in response to the threat of disapproval from parents. Both anxieties can carry over into the life of the adult only child who, in marriage, can find social or emotional distance and criticism from a partner very threatening.

What can amplify the power of these anxieties is fear on either side, the parents' or the child's, with the fear of one increasing fear in the other. Thus a young child who is anxious about starting school can be made more so by parents who are anxious about letting him go. One of the most painful separation anxieties is homesickness (a psychological complaint often accompanied by physical symptoms), which requires empathetic support and parental firmness to resolve. This separation challenge is associated not just with entering elementary school but also with graduating from high school as well when the adolescent fears living apart from family.

Now issues of the empty nest—leaving it for the adolescent, living in it for the parents—must be handled by parents with confidence and care—supporting the child's departure while assuring her of their care. Later, another major separation looms when the adult only child commits to a life partner and must reconcile this primary attachment with the historical attachment to parents, who have to learn to gladly share their grown child with this new love.

Differentiation anxiety goes to the heart of adolescent development, challenging the only child to dare parental disapproval through enough healthy experimentation so she can claim an identity she can honestly call her own. What I sometimes see in adult only children are extremely well individuated people with a strong personality, but often not very well differentiated from the child they once were, from how their parents are, and from how those parents have always wanted her to be. When this happens, conformity to parents can be at the expense of potential development and personal growth.

A FINAL WORD

ACCEPTANCE

A Matter of Appreciation

In preparing to write *The Future of Your Only Child,* I read many books about only children. Not surprisingly, most were by writers who are parents of an only child or are an only child themselves. Amply quoted in this book, they are listed in the bibliography, and all are recommended reading because each one has something uniquely helpful and insightful to say about this psychologically complicated childhood, challenge in parenting, and adult outcome. As a final word, I quote from what one of these authors, Darrell Sifford, concludes about his upbringing, his parents, and himself as an adult only child. His statement of acceptance is based on a deep appreciation of the complicated journey that he and his parents have taken together.

I better understand now why I sometimes take myself too seriously, why I don't always laugh when the joke's on me, why it's important for me to be recognized as special and to be treated that way, why I'm sometimes accused of acting like a retired Army colonel, why I attach myself so strongly to a few people and a few things and how losing them plays into my only-child fears of abandonment. I better understand now why I enjoy solitude, why I struggle during holidays when I'm thrown together with my wife's vast extended family, why I'm fundamentally a solo act rather than a team player. I better understand my parents and their wounds and why they treated me as they did. I think I appreciate myself more now, too, although the

few people who knew me really well may wonder if that's possible. I
think I'll be able to extend myself more to other people, to be more
giving, accepting, understanding. I think I'm getting closer to being
a more complete person, more open and less defended.

The writer goes on to say,

If there is one message I want to leave with only children . . . it is
this: Only children need to understand how much they mean to
their parents, how most of whatever happened in the growing-up
process was built on what was intended to be pure love and healthy
expectation. I think that only children, more than other children,
can be healed by acceptance of parents as people who did the best
they could with what they had to work with. We can ask no more
of anybody, including ourselves.[1]

I second what this writer says and add that I hope you enjoy your
only child if you are a parent, and appreciate being an only child if
you are now an adult.

APPENDIX A

SELF-MANAGEMENT FOR ADULT ONLY CHILDREN

These guidelines are derived from J. Pitkeathley and D. Emerson, "The Ten-Point Survival Plan," *Only Child* (1994), pp. 228–229.

1. It is better to accept yourself for being human than to blame yourself for not being perfect.
2. It is better to treat yourself kindly during hard times than to beat up on yourself when things go wrong.
3. It is better to laugh at yourself than to take yourself too seriously.
4. It is better to appreciate the good in other people than to criticize them for not living up to your expectations.
5. It is better to celebrate the strengths from growing up as an only child than to regret the limitations.
6. It is better to achieve for your personal satisfaction than to prove your self-worth.
7. It is better to refuse requests that feel excessive than to automatically say "yes" and over do.
8. It is better to express your insecure side than to maintain the pretense that you are nothing but strong.

9.   It is better to limit responsibility to your own decisions than to help others by taking responsibility for theirs.

10.   It is better to show consideration for others than to be only concerned with yourself.

APPENDIX B

NOTABLE ONLY CHILDREN

As parents wondering about the future of your only child, it can be fun to identify a few grown only children who turned out to be achievers in some popular or historical way. Here are some to consider.

Hans Christian Andersen
Alvin Ailey
Lauren Bacall
Erma Bombeck
Fernando Bujones
Carol Channing
Sammy Davis Jr.
Thomas Alva Edison
Indira Ghandi

Lena Horne
Elton John
John Lennon
Joe Montana
Isaac Newton
Elvis Presley
Buffy Sainte-Marie
Leonardo da Vinci
Oprah Winfrey

FURTHER READING

Bregue, Laurent and Sebastian Roché. "Birth Order and Youth Delinquent Behavior: Testing the Differential Parental Control Hypothesis in a French Representative Sample." *Psychology, Crime and Law* 11, no. 1 (March 2005), pp. 73–85.

Bradshaw, John. *Bradshaw On: The Family.* Deerfield Beach, Fla.: HCI, 1990.

Coates, Anne. *Your Only Child.* London: Bloomsbury, 1996.

Cutts, Norma E., and Nicholas Mosely. *The Only Child: A Guide for Parents.* New York: G. P Putnam's Sons, 1954.

Engler, Barbara. *Personality Theories.* Boston: Houghton Mifflin, 1999.

Ernst, Cecilé. "In Expectation of Meta-Analysis." *Politics and the Life Sciences* 19, no. 2 (September 2000), p. 150 – 160.

Goleman, Daniel. *Social Intelligence.* New York: Bantam, 2006.

Hertz, Rosanna. *Single by Chance, Mothers by Choice: How Women Are Choosing Parenthood Without Marriage and Creating the New American Family.* New York: Oxford University Press, 2006.

Howard, Margo. *A Life in Letters: Ann Landers' Letters to Her Only Child.* New York: Warner Books, 2003.

Isaacson, Cliff, and Kris Radish. *The Birth Order Effect.* Avon, Mass.: Adams Media, 2002.

Jones, Charlotte Foltz. *Only Child: Clues for Coping.* Philadelphia: Westminster Press, 1984.

Leman, Kevin. *The Birth Order Book: Why You Are the Way You Are.* Grand Rapids, Mich.: Revell, 1998.

Manassis, Katharina. *Keys to Parenting Your Anxious Child.* Hauppauge, N.Y.: Barron's Educational Series, 1996.

McGrath, Ellie. *My One and Only: The Special Experience of the Only Child.* New York: William Morrow, 1989.

Montgomery, Sy. *The Good Pig: The Extraordinary Life of Christopher Hogwood.* New York: Ballantine Books, 2006.

Murano, Hara Estroff. "Singletons at Risk?" *Psychology Today.* March/April 2007, pp. 50 – 51.

Nachman, Patricia A., and Andrea Thompson. *You and Your Only Child: The Joys, Myths, and Challenges of Raising an Only Child.* New York: HarperPerennial, 1997.

Newman, Susan. *Parenting an Only Child: The Joys and Challenges of Raising Your One and Only.* New York: Broadway Books, 1990.

O'Connor, Frank. *An Only Child and My Father's Son.* New York: Penguin Group, 2005.

Paulhus, Delroy L., Paul Wehr, and Paul D. Trapnell. "Resolving Controversy over Birth Order and Personality: By Debate or Design?" *Politics and the Life Sciences* 19, no. 2 (September 2000), pp. 177 – 179.

Peck, Ellen. *The Joy of the Only Child.* New York: Delacorte Press, 1977.

Pickhardt, Carl. *The Everything Parent's Guide to Positive Discipline.* Avon, Mass.: Adams Media, 2004.

———. *The Everything Parent's Guide to the Strong-Willed Child.* Avon, Mass.: Adams Media, 2005.

———. *The Trout King: A Novel About Fathers and Sons.* Philadelphia: Xlibris, 2005. About parenting an only child son.

———. *The Art Lover: About the Love of Art and the Art of Love.* New York/Lincoln/Shanghai: iUniverse, 2006. About parenting an only child daughter.

———. *The Everything Parent's Guide to Children and Divorce.* Avon, Mass.: Adams Media, 2006.

———. *The Helper's Apprentice: The Jackson Skye Mysteries.* New York/Lincoln/ Shanghai: iUniverse, 2006. A fictional textbook of real-life problems for young people growing up.

———. *The Connected Father: Understanding Your Unique Role and Responsibilities During Your Child's Adolescence.* New York: Palgrave Macmillan, 2007.

Pitkeathley, Jill and David Emerson. *Only Child: How to Survive Being One.* London: Souvenir Press, 1994.

Polit, Denise F. and Toni Falbo. "Only Children and Personality Development: A Quantitative Review." *Journal of Marriage and Family* 49, no. 2 (May 1987), pp. 309 – 325.

Pollock, David C. *Third Culture Kids: The Experience of Growing Up among Worlds.* London: Nicholas Brealey Publishing, 2001.

Shyer, Marlene Fanta. *Here I Am, an Only Child.* New York: Aladdin Books, Macmillan, 1987.

Siegel, Deborah, and Daphne Uviller, eds. *Only Child: Writers on the Singular Joys and Solitary Sorrows Growing Up Solo.* New York: Harmony Books, 2006.

Sifford, Darrell. *The Only Child: Being One, Loving One, Understanding One, Raising One.* New York: Harper and Row, 1989.

Sulloway, Frank J. *Born to Rebel: Birth Order, Family Dynamics, and Creative Lives.* New York: Random House, 1997.

Toman, Walter. *Family Constellation: Its Effects on Personality and Social Behavior.* New York: Springer, 1993.

White, Carolyn. *The Seven Common Sins of Parenting an Only Child: A Guide for Parents and Families.* San Francisco: Jossey-Bass, 2004.

Woititz, Janet. *Adult Children of Alcoholics.* Deerfield Beach, Fla.: HCI, 1990.

Zimmerman, Jeffrey, and Elizabeth S. Thayer, *Adult Children of Divorce: How to Overcome the Legacy of Your Parents' Breakup and Enjoy Love, Trust, and Intimacy.* Oakland, Calif.: New Harbinger Publications, 2003.

NOTES

Unless otherwise attributed, all quotations used are fictional, created to reflect concerns similar in kind to those that clients have expressed to me in counseling over the years. Any resemblance to real persons or situations is purely coincidental.

INTRODUCTION

1. John Bradshaw, *Bradshaw On: The Family* (Deerfield Beach, Fla.: HCI, 1990), p. 1.
2. David C. Pollock, *Third Culture Kids: The Experience of Growing Up Among Worlds* (London: Nicholas Brealey Publishing, 2001), p. 5.
3. Jeffrey Zimmerman and Elizabeth S. Thayer, *Adult Children of Divorce: How to Overcome the Legacy of Your Parents' Breakup and Enjoy Love, Trust, and Intimacy* (Oakland, Calif.: New Harbinger Publications, 2003), p. 44.
4. Janet Woititz, *Adult Children of Alcoholics* (Deerfield Beach, Fla.: HCI, 1990), p. 86.
5. Jill Pitkeathley and David Emerson, *Only Child: How to Survive Being One* (London: Souvenir Press, 1994), p. 177.
6. Darrell Sifford, *The Only Child: Being One, Loving One, Understanding One, Raising One* (New York: Harper and Row, 1989), pp. 23–24.
7. Norma E. Cutts and Nicholas Mosely, *The Only Child: A Guide for Parents* (New York: G. P. Putnam's Sons, 1954), p. 10.
8. Pitkeathley and Emerson, p. 235.
9. Susan Newman, *Parenting an Only Child: The Joys and Challenges of Raising Your One and Only* (New York: Broadway Books, 1990), p. 181.
10. Ellen Peck, *The Joy of the Only Child* (New York: Delacorte Press, 1977), p. 9.
11. Ibid., p. 54.

CHAPTER 1: BIRTH ORDER AND ONLY-CHILD RESEARCH

1. Frank J. Sulloway, *Born to Rebel: Birth Order, Family Dynamics, and Creative Lives* (New York: Random House, 1997), p. 22.
2. Cindy Kranz, "One Child No Longer a Lonely Number," *Cincinnati Inquirer,* June 30, 2000.
3. Michele M. Melendez, "With More Families Opting for Just One Child, the 'Only' Stigma Is Fading," *Newhouse News Service,* May 7, 2005.

4.   *FamilyEducation.com,* September 2006.

5.   *American Demographics,* November 1, 2001.

6.   Cliff Isaacson and Kris Radish, *The Birth Order Effect* (Avon, Mass.: Adams Media, 2002), p. 70.

7.   Cecilé Ernst, "In Expectation of Meta-Analysis," *Politics and the Life Sciences* 19, no. 2 (September 2000), p. 159–160.

8.   Sulloway, p. xiv.

9.   Lauren Beche and Sebastian Roché, "Birth Order and Youth Delinquent Behavior: Testing the Differential Parental Control Hypothesis in a French Representative Sample," *Psychology, Crime and Law* 11, no. 1 (March 2005), pp. 73–85.

10. Delroy L. Paulhaus, Paul Wehr, and Paul D. Trapnell, "Resolving Controversy over Birth Order and Personality: By Debate or Design?" *Politics and the Life Sciences* 19, no. 2 (September 2000), pp. 177 – 179.

11. Sulloway, p. xiv.

12. Ibid., pp. 21–22,

13. Ibid., p. 69.

14. Ibid., p. 70.

15. Ibid., p. 73.

16. Barbara Engler, *Personality Theories* (Boston: Houghton Mifflin, 1999), p. 102.

17. Denise Polit and Toni Falbo, "Only Children and Personality Development: A Quantitative Review," *Journal of Marriage and the Family* 49, no. 2 (May 1987), p. 309.

18. Toni Falbo, "Your One and Only," *University of Texas College of Education News,* July 20, 2004. Accessed at www.edb.utexas.edu/education/news/2004/Falbo0704.php.

19. Walter Toman, *Family Constellation: Its Effects on Personality and Social Behavior* (New York: Springer, 1993), pp. 25–27.

20. Pitkeathley and Emerson, p. 4.

CHAPTER 2: ATTENTION

1.   Deborah Siegel and Daphne Uviller, eds., *Only Child: Writers on the Singular Joys and Solitary Sorrows Growing Up Solo* (New York: Harmony Books, 2006), pp. 224–229.

2.   Patricia Nachman and Andrea Thompson, *You and Your Only Child: The Joys, Myths, and Challenges of Raising an Only Child* (New York: HarperPerennial, 1997), pp. 73–83.

3.   Newman, p. 236.

4.   Charlotte Foltz Jones, *Only Child: Clues for Coping* (Philadelphia: Westminster Press, 1984), p. 103.

5.   Ellie McGrath, *My One and Only: The Special Experience of the Only Child* (New York: William Morrow, 1989), p. 151.

6.   Carolyn White, *The Seven Common Sins of Parenting an Only Child: A Guide for Parents and Families* (San Francisco: Jossey-Bass, 2004), p. 27.

7.   Sifford, pp. 136–137.

8.   Siegel and Uviller, p. 84.

9.   McGrath, p. 49.

10. Ibid., pp. 48–49.

11. Newman, p. 117.

12. Pitkeathley and Emerson, p. 50.

13. Ibid., p. 69.

14. Newman, p. 117.
15. Seigel and Uviller, p. 112.
16. Pitkeathley and Emerson, p. 203.
17. White, pp. 71–71.
18. Newman, p. 120.

CHAPTER 3: SENSITIVITY

1. Newman, p. 112.
2. Pitkeathley and Emerson, p. 76.
3. Newman, p. 166.
4. Pitkeathley and Emerson, p. 253.
5. Ibid.
6. Sifford, p. 175.
7. Nachman and Thompson, p.169.
8. Pitkeathley and Emerson, p. 106.
9. Sifford, p. 101.

CHAPTER 4: CONSTANCY

1. Isaacson and Radish, p. 201.
2. Pitkeathley and Emerson, p. 118.
3. Sulloway, p. 23.
4. Ibid., p. 70.
5. Katharina Manassis, *Keys to Parenting Your Anxious Child* (Hauppauge, N.Y.: Barron's Educational Series, 1996), p. 72.
6. Carl Pickhardt, *The Everything Parent's Guide to Children and Divorce* (Avon, Mass.: Adams Media, 2006), p. 37.
7. Carl Pickhardt, *The Connected Father: Understanding Your Unique Role and Responsibilities During Your Child's Adolescence* (New York: Palgrave Macmillan, 2007), chap. 5.
8. McGrath, pp. 100–101.
9. Cutts and Mosely, pp. 15–16.
10. Isaacson and Radish, p. 51.
11. Ibid., p. 62.
12. Peck, p.111.
13. Isaacson and Radish, p. 62.

CHAPTER 5: FRIENDSHIP

1. Jones, pp. 60–62.
2. McGrath, 1989, p. 129.
3. Isaacson and Radish, p. 54.
4. Siegel and Uviller, p. 175.
5. Sifford, p. 12.
6. Siegel and Uviller, p.112.
7. Ibid., p.123.
8. Ibid., p. 129.
9. Nachman and Thompson, p. 78.

10. Newman, p.174.
11. Sifford, p. 17.
12. Nachman and Thompson, p. 95.
13. Jones, pp. 50–51.
14. Peck, p. 5.
15. McGrath, p. 45.
16. Anne Coates, *Your Only Child* (London: Bloomsbury, 1996), p. 127.
17. Newman, p. 158.
18. Hara Estroff Murano, "Singletons at risk?" *Psychology Today,* March/April 2007, pp. 50–51.
19. Coates, p. 48.
20. McGrath, p. 195.
21. Siegel and Uviller, pp. 135–139.
22. Ibid., p. 147.
23. McGrath, p. 219.
24. Jones, p. 45.

CHAPTER 6: WILLFULNESS

1. Carl Pickhardt, *The Everything Parent's Guide to the Strong-Willed Child* (Avon, Mass.: Adams Media, 2005), p. v.
2. Ibid., p. 21.
3. McGrath, p. 149.
4. White, p. 12.
5. Ibid., p. 62.
6. Pickhardt, *Positive Discipline,* p. v.
7. Sifford, pp. 141–142.
8. Coates, p. 92.
9. Jones, p. 96. Emphasis added.
10. Newman, p. 237.
11. Peck, p. 59.
12. Pickhardt, *Strong-Willed Child,* pp. 72–73.
13. Margo Howard, *A Life in Letters: Ann Landers' Letters to Her Only Child* (New York: Warner Books, 2003), pp. 14, 108, 257.
14. Nachman and Thompson, p. 98.
15. Ibid., p. 119.
16. Pitkeathley and Emerson, p. 123.
17. McGrath, pp. 138–139.
18. Coates, p. 107.
19. Sy Montgomery, *The Good Pig: The Extraordinary Life of Christopher Hogwood* (New York: Ballantine Books, 2006), pp. 17–18.
20. McGrath, pp. 149–158.

CHAPTER 7: ATTACHMENT

1. Peck, p. 101.
2. Newman, pp. 61–62.

3. *AARP Magazine,* January/February 2007, p. 36. Emphasis added.
4. Daniel Goleman, *Social Intelligence* (New York: Bantam, 2006), pp. 20–26.
5. Marlene Fanta Shyer, *Here I Am, an Only Child* (New York: Aladdin Books, Macmillan, 1987), p. 14.
6. Isaacson and Radish, pp. 56–57.
7. Cutts and Mosely, p. 11.
8. Newman, p. 99.
9. Siegel and Uviller, p. 39.
10. White, pp.143–144.
11. Nachman and Thompson, pp. 121–123.
12. Newman, p. 57.
13. Cutts and Mosely, p. 22.
14. Pickhardt, *Children and Divorce,* pp. 237–238.
15. Newman, p. 84.
16. Coates, p. 124.
17. Jones, pp. 31–32.
18. Nachman and Thompson, pp. 206–209.
19. Jones, p. 51.
20. Pitkeathley and Emerson, p. 245.
21. McGrath, p. 194.
22. Sifford, p. 170.

CHAPTER 8: CONFLICT

1. McGrath, pp. 110–111.
2. Nachman and Thompson, p. 58.
3. Pitkeathley and Emerson, p. 170.
4. Nachman and Thompson, pp. 133–134.
5. Goleman, p. 175.
6. White, p. 155.
7. Pitkeathley and Emerson, pp.72–73.
8. Ibid., pp. 188–191.
9. Ibid., p. 252.
10. Sifford, pp. 195–201.

CHAPTER 9: RECTITUDE

1. Pitkeathley and Emerson, p. 155.
2. Peck, p. 4.
3. Ibid., pp. 114–115.
4. Newman, p. 66.
5. Sulloway, p. 69
6. Sifford, pp. 187–188.
7. Kevin Leman, *The Birth Order Book: Why You Are the Way You Are* (Grand Rapids, Mich.: Revell, 1998), pp. 130–137.
8. Sulloway, p. 161.

CHAPTER 10: AMBITION

1. Howard, p. xii.
2. Ibid., p. 2.
3. Ibid., p. 57.
4. Sifford, p. 166.
5. White, p. 120.
6. Nachman and Thompson, p. 84.
7. Newman, p. 242.
8. Jones, p. 99.
9. Tony Falbo, quoted in McGrath, pp. 174–175.
10. Cutts and Mosely, p. 90.
11. Carl Pickhardt, *The Helper's Apprentice: The Jackson Skye Mysteries* (New York/Lincoln/Shanghai: iUniverse, 2006), p. 315.
12. Manassis, p. 122.
13. Siegel and Uviller, p. 190.
14. Pitkeathley and Emerson, p. 171.
15. Ibid., p. 274.
16. Leman, p. 117.

CHAPTER 11: RESPONSIBILITY

1. Carl Pickhardt, *The Everything Parent's Guide to Positive Discipline* (Avon, Mass.: Adams Media, 2004), pp. 25–26.
2. Ibid., pp. 26 – 27.
3. Siegel and Uviller, p. 5.
4. White, p. 37. Emphasis added.
5. Ibid., p. 41.
6. Cutts and Mosely, pp. 120–126.
7. McGrath, p. 147.
8. Ibid., p. 161.
9. Ibid., p. 212.
10. Pitkeathley and Emerson, pp. 38–39.

CHAPTER 12: POSSESSIVENESS

1. McGrath, p. 156.
2. Coates, p. 63.
3. Shyer, p. 27.
4. McGrath, p. 194.
5. Pitkeathley and Emerson, p. 191.
6. Ibid., pp. 237–239.
7. Sifford, p. 16.
8. Nachman and Thompson, p. 57.
9. Peck, p. 47.
10. McGrath, p. 104.
11. Pitkeathley and Emerson, pp. 63–64.

12. Ibid., pp. 65–70.

CHAPTER 13: APPROVAL

1. McGrath, p. 91.
2. Siegel and Uviller, p. 96.
3. Coates, p. 66.
4. White, p. 159.
5. Nachman and Thompson, pp. 154–155.
6. White, p. 163.
7. Cutts and Mosely, p. 91.
8. Sifford, p. 113.

CHAPTER 14: DEPENDENCE

1. Coates, p. 83.
2. Nachman and Thompson, p. 49.
3. Foltz Jones, p. 78.
4. Coates, pp. 83–90.
5. Peck, pp.82–84.
6. Newman, p. 157.
7. Cutts and Mosely, pp. 22–23.
8. McGrath, p. 147.
9. Ibid., p. 147.
10. Ibid., p. 148.
11. Pitkeathley and Emerson, pp. 120–121.
12. Sifford, p. 158.
13. Ibid., p. 161.

CHAPTER 15: PRESSURE

1. Cutts and Mosely, pp. 11–13.
2. Anonymous Internet posting, accessed 11/10/07 at www.realjokes.net/viewjoke153 .html.
3. Nachman and Thompson, pp. 145 – 146.
4. White, pp. 115–116.
5. McGrath, pp. 176–177.
6. Peck, p. 156.
7. Pitkeathley and Emerson, pp. 26–39.
8. Sifford, p. 56.
9. Nachman and Thompson, p. 12.
10. Newman, pp. 144–147. Emphasis added.

CHAPTER 16: ANXIETY

1. Foltz Jones, p. 76.
2. Cutts and Mosely, pp. 159–161.

3. Peck, p. 114.
4. Pitkeathley and Emerson, p. 91.
5. Ibid., p. 112.
6. Ibid., p. 170.
7. B. G. Rosenberg, "Birth Order and Personality: Is Sulloway's Treatment a Radical Rebellion or Is He Preserving the Status Quo?" *Politics and the Life Sciences* 19, no. 2 (September 2000), p. 171. Emphasis added.
8. Sulloway, p. 97.
9. Ibid., p. 98.
10. White, p. 114.
11. Sifford, p. 172.
12. McGrath, p. 91.
13. Ibid., p. 166.

A FINAL WORD: ACCEPTANCE

1. Sifford, pp. 220–221.

INDEX